Themed Sermon Illustrations

An abundance of gems to drop into your talk

David Adam

kevin mayhew

kevin mayhew

First published in Great Britain in 2011 by Kevin Mayhew Ltd
Buxhall, Stowmarket, Suffolk IP14 3BW
Tel: +44 (0) 1449 737978 Fax: +44 (0) 1449 737834
E-mail: info@kevinmayhewltd.com
Web: www.kevinmayhew.com

Themed Sermon Illustrations is extracted from *Searchlights*.

ISBN 978 1 84867 336 6
Catalogue No 1501255

Cover design by Rob Mortonson
© Image copyright Dan Gerber
Used under licence from Shutterstock Inc.

Printed in Great Britain

Contents

About the author		9
Introduction		10
Advent and Christmas		
1.	Waiting for God	13
2.	Stir-up Sunday	15
3.	Ready for Christmas	16
4.	God's gift	17
5.	Seeing clearly	18
6.	A free gift	19
7.	Wise men	20
Lent and Easter		
8.	Weeding and pruning	23
9.	Lazy Jack	24
10.	Victory	25
11.	The breath of life	26
12.	The light of life	27
13.	The living Lord	28
14.	New air	29
Mothering Sunday		
15.	Thanks, Mum	33
16.	A mother's love	34
God with us		
17.	Be prepared	37
18.	Heaven here and now	38
19.	God who protects us	39
20.	Trust in God	40
21.	God's glory revealed	41
22.	Meeting the risen Lord	42
23.	At all times and in all places	43
24.	God with us	44

25. God cares for us 45
26. The storms of life 46
27. God's love is not exclusive 47
28. Not what, but whom 48
29. Good News in dark times 49
30. Walk in the light 50
31. New every morning 51
32. God around us 52
33. The Good Shepherd 53
34. Rescued from above 54
35. Sufficient energy 55
36. The power of the Lord 56
37. The gift of the kingdom 57
38. Seeking the lost 58
39. Shining in the dark 59
40. A faithful helper 60
41. Unity 61
42. Under control 62
43. God waiting and watching 63
44. Letting God in 64
45. The peace of Christ's presence 45
46. God in us 66
47. Who is my neighbour? 67
48. Meeting us where we are 68
49. God in the here and now 69
50. Immersed in God 70
51. A transforming presence 71
52. Seek and find 72
53. Raising us up to God 73
54. Ready and waiting 74
55. Extraordinarily ordinary 75
56. Jesus the Anointed One 76
57. Faith in his presence 77

Prayer
58. Listening 81
59. Charging our batteries 82
60. Contact 83

61. Prayer and hypocrisy 84
62. True love 85
63. Make room for Jesus 86
64. Attentiveness 87
65. Perseverance 88
66. The experience of grace 89
67. Exploring the Lord's Prayer 90
68. Tuned in to God 91
69. Seeking the way 92
70. The power and guidance of the Spirit 93

Love, wealth and happiness
71. Abusing the rules 97
72. Unheeded warning 98
73. The blind leading the blind 99
74. Opportunity 100
75. Love one another 101
76. Jesus fills our emptiness 102
77. Hospitality 103
78. Enough for all 104
79. Forgiveness rebuilds relationships 105
80. The Beatitudes 106
81. Priorities 107
82. Treasuring humanity 108
83. Finding true wealth 109
84. Happiness in giving 110
85. Inner peace and happiness 111
86. Something money can't buy 112
87. The Midas touch 113

Signs of glory
88. Filling a vacuum 117
89. Abundant life 118
90. Light 119
91. Natural healing 120
92. Don't be alarmed 121
93. The glory of the Trinity 122
94. The kingship of Christ 123

95. Jesus shows God's glory 124
96. Celebrating women in mission 125
97. God's love is his glory 126
98. Watching and waiting 127
99. Glorious humility 128

New life in Christ
100. God's transforming power 131
101. Jesus, our light and life 132
102. The resurrection and the life 133
103. Jesus leads his flock 134
104. Jesus is the way 135
105. Father, Son and Holy Spirit 136
106. Transformed by his power 137
107. Responding to Jesus' call 138
108. Forgiveness has no limits 139
109. RSVP 140
110. Love's explosion 141
111. Full or empty? 142
112. Sight restored, life renewed 143
113. God sends and saves 144
114. It's not about appearances 145
115. Christ sets us free 146
116. God's indestructible hope 147
117. Through death to life 148
118. Love brings new life 149
119. From destruction to renewal 150

The life of faith
120. Never put off today… 153
121. Practise what you preach 154
122. Perfect freedom 155
123. Many roads to God 156
124. Bringing others to Jesus 157
125. Giving ourselves to God 158
126. The light of Christ 159
127. The light of the world 160
128. Made in his image 161

129.	Temptation	162
130.	The Prince of Peace	163
131.	Love expressed in action	164
132.	Filled with the Spirit	165
133.	Firm foundations	166
134.	Go out in my name	167
135.	Growing seeds	168
136.	Weeding out the harmful	169
137.	The kingdom of heaven	170
138.	Seek first God's will	171
139.	God's generosity	172
140.	Words and deeds	173
141.	Care for God's world	174
142.	Give God his due	175
143.	Love your neighbour	176
144.	Due care and attention	178
145.	Use it or lose it	179
146.	As you did to the least of these	180
147.	Help is on the way	181
148.	The Promised Land	182
149.	Obeying God's call	183
150.	Good rules	184
151.	Evangelism	185
152.	Oliver's request	186
153.	The greatness of God	187
154.	Risk	188
155.	Sowing seed	189
156.	Freedom	190
157.	Is it worth the effort?	191
158.	Dying of analysis	192
159.	A Godless church	193
160.	Obeying the vision	194
161.	The fourth Wise Man	195
162.	Self-giving	196
163.	Serving the poor	197
164.	Lantern Saints	198
165.	Prayer-based faith	199
166.	Grace is not cheap	200

167. The mission of the seventy 201
168. Dedication and practice 202
169. The communion of saints 203
170. Faith on a cheerless day 204
171. Temptation is everywhere 205
172. Trusting God's promise 206
173. A life of purpose 207
174. Living to God's glory 208
175. Freedom in giving and receiving 209
176. Hearing the Shepherd's voice 210
177. Deepening our relationship with God 211
178. God's gift of peace 212
179. Proclaiming the story 213
180. Humbly open to God 214

Topical index 215
Bible reference index 220
Acknowledgements 224

About the author

David Adam was the Vicar of Lindisfarne, off the Northumbrian coast, for 13 years until he retired in March 2003. His work involved ministering to thousands of pilgrims and other visitors. He is the author of many inspiring books on spirituality and prayer, and his Celtic writings have rekindled a keen interest in our Christian heritage.

Other titles by David Adam:

The Echo of God (Product code: 1501113)
Prayers of Intercession (Product code: 1501051)
The Great 'I Am' (Product code: 1501135)
Looking and Longing (Product code: 1500634)

Introduction

This book of sermon illustrations was compiled with the busy minister, preacher or speaker in mind: it can be a daunting task to find a fresh theme or topic each week and these short pieces will hopefully be a handy resource. They are meant to help provide that sometimes elusive topic or to amplify an existing central theme.

Visual aids often speak more directly than words and these short, vivid illustrations, as well as illustrations from your locality, can help you to throw light on the Scripture passages and to relate them to what is happening in your community or the world. By referring to the two indexes (Topical and Bible reference) you can decide how to plan the sermon or expand on your own theme. The cross-referencing means that you have quite a few ideas at your fingertips.

Advent and Christmas

1 Waiting for God

Aim

To make people more aware that Christ comes to them today.

Reading

Mark 13:35

Illustration

It was near Christmas and in the Advent season, and Peter waited for God to come. He prayed every day, 'God, show me your face and I shall be saved.' Peter had tried to live a good life; he was now old and looked forward to the coming of God. He continued to work in his paper shop, where he had worked most of his life. Here he heard all sorts of conversations and met many people. A single mum was telling a friend how she did not have enough money to buy presents for her child. When everyone else had gone, Peter said to her, 'I heard what you said. I have a few toys on the shelves; they are not selling very well, go and pick anything you would like.' She could hardly believe it for there were some wonderful things on the shelves. As she went away with her arms full, Peter was delighted. His reward was her smile.

Later that day, he caught a young lad stealing a magazine from the shelves. He was on the way out with the magazine up his jumper when Peter stopped him. He could have called the police or told the boy's parents. He saw the boy was poor and afraid, and he felt sorry for him. 'If you want a magazine, and have no money, talk with me,' he said. 'Magazines are soon out of date; I can always find one to give you. You must not just help yourself. Take the magazine for free and ask me another time.' The boy's face changed from a look of fear to a beaming smile. He thanked Peter and ran from the shop.

An old man came into the shop and was saying how lonely he was since his wife died. This would be his first Christmas on his own – he was not looking forward to it. Peter said, 'We were expecting a friend to come for Christmas, and he has said he cannot make it. We have prepared for his coming. Would you come to us instead? We would love to share Christmas with you.' The old man's face lit up in a beautiful smile and he said, 'You have made me feel so wanted, and I would love to come.'

That night Peter prayed his Advent prayer, 'Show me your face and I shall be saved.' In a dream God spoke to him and said, 'Peter, today I came to you, and three times you made me smile. Grace and peace be upon you.'

(Apologies to Tolstoy!)

2 Stir-up Sunday

Aim

To show we need to prepare for the coming of our Lord.

Reading

Mark 1:3

Illustration

The Sunday before the beginning of Advent used to be called 'Stir-up Sunday' for two reasons. The prayer for the Sunday begins, 'Stir up, O Lord, the wills of your faithful people'; a wonderful prayer that wants us to 'bring forth the fruits of good works'. It is by what we do that we will be known, so it is important that our works are good, important that we do something.

Traditionally 'Stir-up Sunday' was also the time when the Christmas cake was made. Mother would get all the ingredients – the flour, the fruit, the eggs – and mix them together. Everyone in the house had a stir of the cake before it went into the oven. All this was part of the preparations before Christmas.

We now often spend weeks preparing for this one day. How much time do we spend preparing for the coming of God to us?

If someone is coming to stay, we will make sure there is room for them, that we have time for them, that we will give them some attention. Our God comes and seeks room in our lives; he wants us to be aware of him, for us to give him some of our time and attention.

Are you prepared for this?

3 Ready for Christmas

Aim

To show God's kingdom comes when his will is done.

Readings

John 2:11
Luke 2:7

Illustration

Are you ready for Christmas? Have you sent all your cards? Bought presents? Got the food ready? What will you do on Christmas Day? Will you make room for Jesus: make sure Christ is in Christ-mas?

It was Jessie's birthday and she looked forward to it. She lived in an old people's home and had friends around her – but she was invited to her daughter's for her birthday. She would be with the family, including the three children. They made sure there was a nice room ready for her and the house was warm. Her daughter had bought the food she liked. All was ready.

On the first night her daughter had an evening class, the children were out with friends, and her son-in-law decided to go to the pub. On her birthday the children had other things to do and so would be out all day – football, swimming and netball are important. Jessie's son-in-law spent the day in the garage tinkering with his car, and her daughter decided to do some last-minute shopping on her own. Again Jessie was left alone. They had a meal together in the evening, then the children went on the computer and the others watched television. Jessie was glad to go back to the home where people had time to talk to her and give their attention to her.

Will we make time for Jesus on his birthday, or will we be too busy doing other things?

4 God's gift

Aim

To rejoice that Jesus Christ has come into the world.

Reading

John 3:16

Illustration

Mother and Father had wrapped up the present in beautiful paper with tinsel and bows. The present was in a big box. For a long time it remained unopened as if their child was frightened of it. Then the paper was taken off and folded up carefully, the present was taken out of the box, and the child played the whole day with the box. The child enjoyed having the box and playing with it. Mother and Father hoped that their child would soon realise what a wonderful present had been given to her . . .

I knew an old lady who was uninterested in presents. Whenever she was given a present, she was very grateful. She always remembered to say, 'Thank you'. But she did not open the gift. In her house I saw a pile of unopened gifts and I felt it was rather strange and sad.

Today I would like to give you all a present of a cheque for one million pounds. But you can only have it on one condition: you are to frame it, to show how generous I am, but not cash it.

Let us get behind the tinsel and the wrappings today and discover God's greatest gift. He gives himself to us. Let us come and give ourselves to him.

5 Seeing clearly

Aim

To show that the people involved in the birth of Jesus were ordinary people involved in an extraordinary event.

Reading

John 1:18

Illustration

Sally was naughty at school. She did not pay attention to what was written on the board, nor was she all that keen on being out in the country because she was not really interested in the flowers or the birds. A beautiful scene did not move her with joy. Starry nights did not fill her with awe. Then it was discovered that Sally was very short-sighted and needed glasses. She had not been able to see what was around her, so her world and her life were restricted by her vision. Once she had glasses the world became a place full of wonder and beauty. She loved going out into the country to enjoy the scenery, to watch the birds and see the flowers. Once Sally saw more clearly, her whole world changed.

6 A free gift

Aim

To encourage people to wonder at the mystery of Christmas.

Reading

Romans 6:23

Illustration

I get tired of letters through the door that say you have been especially chosen – I know that everyone is getting such a letter. Then it tells me I have won £10,000 – whoopee! But the small print says, 'if my number comes up', and the real chances of that are more than a million to one.

God is not like that. God's offer is not gifts (though he does offer us them); he offers himself to us in Jesus Christ our Lord. We do not deserve this; we cannot win it. God has chosen to give himself to us. All we have to do is accept his presence and his love.

7 Wise men

Aim

To show how the Christ was revealed to all nations.

Reading

Matthew 2:1-12

Illustration

The wise men were not all that wise because they went to the wrong place and the wrong person. They went to the capital, Jerusalem, and to King Herod. Fancy asking him, 'Where is he who is to be born King of the Jews?' Herod hadn't a clue but he knew who would know about the Messiah, about the Christ. He asked the chief priests and scribes. They told him, 'In Bethlehem in the land of Judah.' Lucky for the wise men it was only about seven miles away. Herod sent them off and told them to search diligently for the child and to tell him when they had found him. Fortunately, the wise men did not trust Herod or his interest in the Christ child.

We assume there were three because we are told of three gifts. We know that they were rich, foreign and wise, but we do not know that they were kings. The shepherds were ordinary Jews smelling of sheep and probably not able to read or write. These men were different indeed, almost in total contrast. It helps us to see God calls all peoples to come to him – rich and poor, the known and the stranger, simple and wise; all are invited to come to God.

Lent and Easter

8 Weeding and pruning

Aim

To encourage a positive approach to Lent.

Reading

John 15:1-2
1 Corinthians 3:6-9

Illustration

Some people say they like doing what comes naturally. A man let his garden grow naturally and when asked why it was a mess he said, 'I was leaving it to God.' God will not do for us what he has given us the ability to do. If you want a good garden or a good life, you have to work at it. With the garden, if you want flowers it is no use filling the beds with vegetables. You will get out what you put in. You will get more, for you will also get weeds. If you leave your life to run itself, it will also produce weeds. Gardens and life need regular tender loving care.

Lent is a time for looking at what you have and making improvements.

In the garden some plants need splitting to give them more room to grow. You can often give away the extra to someone else. If you do not divide some plants, they will choke themselves. If we do not learn to give, we will do the same. Make room for the new in your life.

There is a constant need to weed and also to prune. Get rid of what hampers growth. Cut back on what has become rank and is taking over.

Learn to work in relationship with the soil and the climate. Learn to work in relationship with God.

Nothing is achieved without effort, without practice, without learning. If you want a good garden you have to give it priority over other things and the same is true of life.

9 Lazy Jack

Aim

To look at the Passion of Christ and beyond to the resurrection.

Reading

John 12:24

Illustration

Lazy Jack was given a sack of grain. His task was to sow the seed for the village so that they would have a harvest in the autumn. Jack looked at the seed. It was golden and beautiful. He thought it would be a shame to bury it in the ground. So he took it home and put it in a cupboard. No one knew that he had not sown the seed. Jack took it easy. It was only later in the year when there were no shoots, no signs of new wheat growing, that the village realised there was something wrong. Obviously the seed was not in the ground. After a search they found it in Lazy Jack's cupboard. The mice had eaten some, but most of it was still intact. Jack had almost allowed a community to starve by not sowing the seed. Like much in our lives, it was a case of use it or lose it. The villagers put the seed in the ground – it was late for sowing but they trusted in the power within the seed to grow and it did. In the end nothing was lost and the harvest was good.

10 Victory

Aim

To rejoice in the resurrection and in the presence of the risen Lord.

Reading

1 Corinthians 15:57

Illustration

Napoleon escaped from his island prison. His armies regathered under the French flag and Europe was plunged into war. The British army under Wellington landed in Belgium and prepared to fight near a small village called Waterloo. There was no way of communicating to England the news except by semaphore. Day after day a man watched from the tower of Winchester Cathedral, peering towards the south coast. On a misty day the watcher received a message: 'Wellington defeated.' The mist came down and a sadness filled Winchester and spread over England. The watcher stayed at his post. After a long while the mist lifted and the message was repeated: 'Wellington defeated.' But now two more words were added and they made a great difference: 'Wellington defeated the French.' The assumed defeat was a victory. A new message sped to London. Bells rang out and flags flew. The message, which seemed one of defeat, was in fact the start of the news of victory. Likewise we must move from the crucifixion to the joy of the resurrection. We are able to proclaim, 'Death is conquered. We are free. Christ has won the victory.'

11 The breath of life

Aim

To share in the wonder of the resurrection.

Readings

1 Corinthians 15:45
John 20:22

Illustration

Suddenly a man fell to the ground. He had stopped breathing and it would not be long before he was totally dead. But help was at hand. Someone was willing to give him mouth-to-mouth resuscitation. They breathed their breath into him, filling his lungs, and then helped his lungs to expel the air and then receive some more breath. This process went on for a while at ten breaths a minute; without it the man would have died. By the time the ambulance came the man was breathing freely on his own. The person had saved his life. Jesus breathes new life into us and gives us eternal life. Jesus defeats death and brings us to eternal life.

(You may be able to get a St John Ambulance person or a paramedic to offer to demonstrate 'Breath of Life' – they also provide a useful card with this title.)

12 The light of life

Aim

To rejoice in the presence of the risen Lord.

Reading

John 8:12

Illustration

Have you ever been caught in the fog? The whole world becomes cold and grey. Vision is greatly restricted. Everything around appears to be dull and damp. Then suddenly there is a shining, an extra amount of light; there is a radiance that begins to appear all around. The sun breaks through and the fog lifts and disappears. The day seems so glorious and bright. This was the experience of the disciples with the resurrection. They shut themselves in and shut the fullness of life out. They were locked in by sorrow and fear. They just wanted to hide. It was then he came. He came because he was needed. He came back from the dead. He came to be with them. He came to guide them. He came to help them. He came to be friends. He came to transform their world. He comes now and he comes to us. He comes to chase away our darkness and fear and to make our world bright.

13 The living Lord

Aim

To enter into the wonder and joy of the resurrection.

Reading

John 20:1-18

Illustration

1066 is a date we all know: the Battle of Hastings. Did you know the Normans nearly lost the battle?

The English were behind a stockade. The Normans twice tried to break through. The second time they were repelled, it was rumoured that their leader was dead. The troops immediately began to lose heart. Soon they would be in headlong flight. William pulled off his helmet and rode among his troops shouting, 'I am alive. I am still alive.' The result was immediate: new courage, new strength of heart and purpose. This time they burst through the stockade and victory was won.

How like the state of the disciples after Good Friday. They had seen Jesus die; they had lost heart. And then, on that Easter morning, Jesus said to Mary, 'Tell them I am still alive.' What a difference his appearing would make to them and to the world.

14 New air

Aim

To celebrate the hope that the resurrection brings.

Reading

John 20:19-21

Illustration

As a result of an explosion a small group of miners were trapped underground in a confined area. The phone to the surface still worked and they indicated they were all alive but they feared there was not enough air. It was realised that they would die without help – instant help. There was not much hope of getting them out alive. There were tons of earth to be removed and it was calculated it would be too late by the time it was done. With a special drill the rescue team bored a hole to where the men were and then pumped air into the cavern. Though it took another three days to get to them out, the men were found to be well and in good spirits. When one of them was asked what it was like he replied. 'A bit like the resurrection. We were sealed in a tomb unable to get out. Then we were given new air, the breath of life from the air pumped in to us. And then we were rescued and raised into the light.

Mothering Sunday

15 Thanks, Mum

Aim

To help us to appreciate the love that is given to us through our mothers.

Reading

Exodus 20:12

Illustration

By tradition this middle Sunday in Lent was a time when young children who had left home to work in a big house or on a farm were allowed home for the first time in the year. Lots of children had to work for very low wages, sometimes only their keep, and it was very hard. They missed their homes and the care of their mother. At home much had been done for them. Now they had to look after themselves. It was lovely to come home and be looked after and loved. Usually the children had little they could bring as they had little. They may have been allowed to make a cake. More often they would bring a posy of flowers they picked on the way. Perhaps the first time they had thought of giving their mother flowers and saying 'Thank you' for all that their mother had done for them. It is very easy to take our mother for granted and not notice all the work she does for us. She does this work freely, gratis, out of her own grace and goodness. What most of us learn about love, grace and goodness has its foundation in our own homes.

Do you know how much a cup of tea or coffee costs in a café? How much is a meal? What would it cost you to hire a servant to clean for you? Our mother does all this out of love. We should show we appreciate all she does and that we are truly grateful. We should never take our mother for granted or make her work more difficult. As we grow we should know we have a share in that work, because as she loves us, we love her.

16 A mother's love

Aim

To give thanks for all who love us, especially our mothers.

Readings

Luke 2:33-35
John 19:25b-27

Illustration

In J. K. Rowling's story of *Harry Potter and the Philosopher's Stone,* Quirrell, who is working for the wicked Voldemort, tries to kill Harry but is unable to do so even when he uses all the evil powers available to him. Harry asks Professor Dumbledore why Quirrell couldn't touch him and Dumbledore replies that Harry's mother died to save him, and if there was one thing Voldemort couldn't understand it was love. Love as powerful as hers for Harry left its own mark. Not a visible sign . . . but to have been loved so deeply, even though the person who loved us is gone, will give us some protection for ever.

God with us

17 Be prepared

Aim

To prepare for the coming of the Lord.

Reading

Matthew 3:1-12

Illustration

Making a journey was not easy in biblical times. An eastern proverb goes, 'There are three states of misery: illness, fasting and travel.' Before anyone went on a journey they were advised to 'pay all debts, provide for dependants, provide parting gifts, return all articles under trust, take money and a good temper, then bid farewell to all'. Roads were often in poor condition, full of holes and bumps that made travel difficult if not dangerous. Journeying was never done for pleasure. There were few cared-for roads. Josephus tells us that King Solomon laid a causeway of black basalt stone along the roads that led to Jerusalem 'to manifest the grandeur of his riches and government'. All surfaces and built-up roads were originally built for the king and for his use. Before the king was due to visit an area, the inhabitants were visited and warned to be ready. They had to make sure the road didn't have any obstacles to make the king's journey difficult. They also had to be prepared to welcome him. John the Baptist is to be seen as one who tells us of the need to prepare the way for the coming of the King, of the Christ.

18 Heaven here and now

Aim

To rejoice that heaven is not some far-off place but somewhere we should be living in now.

Reading

John 1:(1-9), 10-18

Illustration

A woman from County Kerry in Ireland was asked, 'Where is heaven?' She thought for a moment and then replied, 'About one foot and six inches above me.' She wanted to show that God and heaven are always close at hand and not beyond our reach. We have to just stretch ourselves, extend our vision, give the kingdom of heaven some priority in our life to begin to realise we are there. By giving time and attention to God we learn that 'we dwell in him and he in us'.

19 God who protects us

Aim

To show that God protects us in times of danger.

Reading

Matthew 2:13-23

Illustration

There are many stories of how people have been protected by angels; this one is from Vanuatu (the New Hebrides). The Reverend John Paton went as a missionary to the Hebridean Islands. One night a group of hostile natives surrounded his mission and home. Paton prayed for God to protect him. When morning came Paton was amazed to see his attackers leaving. About a year later the chief accepted Christianity and became a believer. The Reverend John asked him why they had not attacked his house and burned it down. The chief in turn asked him, 'Who were those men you had with you there?'

John replied, 'There were no men, only my wife and I.' The chief argued that he saw many men, big men in shining white garments with drawn swords standing guard.

20 Trust in God

Aim

To encourage a deeper trust in God and to stop worrying.

Reading

Matthew 6:25-34

Illustration

Imagine two people going for a walk together. Both have a difficult task to perform later in the day: a task that will take all their energy and ability.

One man cannot get it out of his mind. He turns it over and over. He does not notice the sunshine or the birds singing. He fails to notice the beauty that is all around him. He may as well be indoors and working.

The other man relaxes for a while in the sunshine. He enjoys the heat of the sun and the sound of the birds. He is aware of the good things around him. He watches a butterfly with delight. This man is being refreshed and restored, ready for the work ahead.

One carried his worries and they wore him down. The other took time off and was refreshed for the job ahead. It is too easy to let worry and anxiety prevent us from enjoying the present moment and steal any energy we have.

21 God's glory revealed

Aim

To show that God reveals his glory in his Son Jesus Christ.

Reading

Matthew 17:1-9

Illustration

As dark clouds cover the sun, so it is easy to let the dark events of life hide from us the glory and the presence of our God. It is then we need know that, even when we lose our grip, we are in the hand of God and in the heart of his Son who says to us, 'Arise, do not be afraid.'

You might like to affirm the words written by a Jewish prisoner on a wall in Cologne:

> I believe in the sun even when it is not shining.
> I believe in love even when I cannot feel it.
> I believe in God even when he is silent.

22 Meeting the risen Lord

Aim

To show that we meet Jesus the risen Lord in various ways.

Reading

Luke 24:13-35

Illustration

The Church in the Outer Hebrides rejoiced in the living Lord who could be met on the road and in the guise of a stranger. The following is an old poem from the Hebrides and now used by the Iona Community:

> I saw a stranger at yestere'en.
> I put food in the eating place,
> drink in the drinking place,
> music in the listening place,
> and in the sacred name of the Triune
> he blessed myself and my house,
> my cattle and my dear ones,
> and the lark said in her song,
> 'Often, often, often,
> goes the Christ in the stranger's guise;
> often, often, often,
> goes the Christ in the stranger's guise.'

23 At all times and in all places

Aim

To affirm that the presence of the ascended Lord is always with us.

Reading

Luke 24:44-53

Illustration

If the disciples were asked after the ascension, 'Where is Jesus now?' their reply would be very like the one that Longinus made to the wife of Pilate in John Masefield's *The Trial of Jesus*. Procula asks, 'Do you think he is dead?' To which Longinus replies, 'No, lady, I don't.' When asked, 'Then where is he?' Longinus replies, 'Let loose in all the world, lady.'

In the ascension we come to know that the Jesus who was limited by time and space is now able to be with all peoples at all times and in all places.

24 God with us

Aim

To show that eternal life comes from abiding in God and knowing he abides in us.

Reading

John 17:(1-11), 20-26

Illustration

In his diary for 1922 Shackleton writes of his Antarctic expedition:

> When I look back on those days, with all their anxiety and peril, I cannot doubt that our party was divinely guided both over snowfield and across storm-swept sea . . . I know that during that long racking march of thirty-six hours over unnamed mountains and glaciers of Southern Georgia it seemed to me we were not three but four. I said nothing to my companions on the point but afterwards Worsley said to me, 'Boss, I had a curious feeling in the march that there was another person with us.'

Do we affirm in our lives that our Lord is with us and travels with us wherever we go?

25 God cares for us

Aim

To show how God cares for us, and how this should drive away fear.

Reading

Matthew 10:24-39

Illustration

Because Jesus says we need to fear God, he adds the balance of the fact that God values us and loves us. He talks of the sparrows in today's reading: 'Are not two sparrows sold for a penny? Yet not one of them falls to the ground without God noticing.' St Luke gives this in a slightly different form: 'Are not five sparrows sold for two pennies? Yet not one of them is forgotten in God's sight.'

It would seem if the buyer was willing to buy four sparrows for two pence, a fifth was thrown in for free. It was as if the sparrow had no value at all! But God noticed and cared; God cares for all his creation.

When Jesus talks of one falling to the ground, it is easy to think of its death, and most people would not notice. But it may just mean land on the ground, to descend from flying. If God notices the small action of the sparrow, will he not all the more care for us?

26 The storms of life

Aim

To show that our God cares and is with us in the storms of life.

Reading

Matthew 14:22-33

Illustration

At lifeboat stations there is usually a record of rescues and of the wonderful bravery of those who went out in the storms to help others. Sometimes, instead of a record of rescue, it simply says, 'Standing by'. That is when the lifeboat was there and ready to help if needed. The crew were keeping a watch and were ready to come to the aid of a troubled vessel if called to do so. How often our God is like that – 'standing by', always ready to help those who call upon him.

Julian of Norwich lived through stormy times. It was the time of the Black Death, the Peasants' Revolt, the battles of Crécy, Poitiers and Agincourt. She saw four kings sit on the throne of England. As a young woman, she had nearly died but she could write:

He did not say, 'You shall not be tempest-tossed; you shall not be work-weary; you shall not be distressed.' But he did say, 'You shall not be overcome.'

Julian was deeply aware that God is 'our maker, our lover and our keeper'. Amidst the storms of life, Julian was aware of the presence, the love and the power of God.

We need to learn to put our hand into the hand of God who never leaves us or forsakes us.

27 God's love is not exclusive

Aim

To show that God's love is not exclusive but is offered to all people, in all places and at all times.

Reading

Matthew 15:(10-20), 21-28

Illustration

We may hate what a person does but we need to learn not to hate the person. It is said that God hates sin but loves the sinner. The more exclusive we become in our dealings, the smaller our world and our heart. God's love is not exclusive.

There is a story of a young man who tried to join a famous London club. He had tried for months and was refused entry for one reason or another. The club was determined to be exclusive. The man's background, place of schooling, position in society did not suit. He was a good man but firmly kept out. In his prayers he asked why this was so. Then, in a vision one night, Jesus came and spoke to him and said, 'I would not worry, you have tried for months to get in; I have tried for years and they have kept me out!' See Matthew 25:45. Consider Edwin Markham's words:

> He drew a circle that shut me out –
> Rebel, heretic, thing to flout.
> But love and I had the wit to win –
> We drew a circle and brought him in.

28 Not what, but whom

Aim

To show that Jesus is the Christ, our Saviour.

Reading

Matthew 16:13-20

Illustration

Many people ask 'What do you believe in?' but for Christians it is not whatbut whom. We believe in the living Christ. We believe that Jesus is the Son of God and is our Saviour. We seek a living relationship with him.

Not what but whom

Not what, but whom, I do believe
that in my darkest hour of need
hath comfort that no mortal creed
to mortal man may give;
not what but whom!
For Christ is more than all the creeds
and his full life of gentle deeds
shall all the creeds outlive.
Not what I do believe but whom!
Who walks beside me in the gloom?
Who shares the burden wearisome?
Who all the dim way doth illume,
and bids me look beyond the tomb
the larger life to live?
Not what I do believe but whom!
Not what, but whom!

John Oxenham

29 Good News in dark times

Aim

To show that our God cares for us in all our troubles and that his kingdom is near.

Reading

Matthew 24:1-14

Illustration

When we have dark or bad days we need to remind ourselves that God is with us and cares for us. Here is a prayer from the Hebrides which you may find helpful:

> Though the dawn breaks cheerless on this Isle today,
> my spirit walks in a path of light.
> For I know my greatness.
> Thou has built me a throne within thy heart.
> I dwell safely within the circle of thy care.
> I cannot for a moment fall out of the everlasting arms.
> I am on my way to thy glory.
> *Hebridean Altars,* Alistair Maclean (1937)

Now that is Good News, whatever the day!

30 Walk in the light

Aim

To rejoice in the light of Christ.

Reading

Ephesians 5:14

Illustration

The illustration today is one of action. We will look to the candle that represents Christ in our midst and we will ask the light of Christ to shine in our lives. Then we will come forward during the singing of a hymn and receive a light.

Have a short silence, then pray:

> Blessed are you, Lord our God,
> for you have called us out of darkness
> into your bright light.
> You have called us to be children of light.
> May the brightness of your presence
> scatter all the darkness that is within us and about us.
> Grant that the lights that we receive
> may remind us of your light
> and of your love towards us,
> Jesus Christ our Lord.
> Amen.

Let everyone come the shortest way to the Christ candle and walk back by going right around the inside of the church.

Sing the hymn 'Walk in the light'.

Let the leader say, 'Receive this light and shine as lights in the world.'

31 New every morning

Aim

To show our God is a healing and forgiving God.

Reading

Lamentations 3:22-23

Illustration

Everybody sing 'Now, every morning is the love'; we need to take it to heart. Read verse 1. We are here awake and alive due to the love of God. During the night we have been refreshed and restored in our powers.

Read verse 2. This verse can change our lives if we take it to heart. 'New perils past': some of the things we feared yesterday did not happen or were not half as bad as we thought. 'New sins forgiven': you need to accept this. What wrongs you did before today are forgiven as long as you intend to lead a new life. You need not carry a great load of guilt around with you; guilt does not change the past but forgiveness changes the future. In the grace and goodness of God you are given a new day – learn to live it. Do not drag old sins and guilt around with you, for they will hamper your life. Start the day anew. Give thanks for the love and the healing power of God in your life. Know you are 'ransomed, healed, forgiven'. Start each day in the presence of God and with new hope in your heart: 'new thoughts of God, new hopes of heaven'.

32 God around us

Aim

To show that Jesus Christ was with the Father before the foundation of the world.

Reading

Acts 17:28

Illustration

There is a fountain in India with fish around it. On the fountain are words by the Indian poet Kabir: 'I laugh if I hear the fish in the sea are thirsty. I laugh if I hear man goes in search of God.'

Just think of a little fish living in a mighty ocean being told its whole life depends on water. One morning it sets out to find water. It leaves its home and travels to cold seas but it cannot find water there. It then travels south to warmer climes, still seeking, but it cannot see water there. It searches all of the seas and all this time it is restless and weary, spending much of its energy. At last it meets an old fish on the seabed and asks, 'Where is the water for I would like some?' 'Do you not know you live in the water, you move in the water, you only exist because of the water? There is no need to look for it, you are in it. If you did not have it you would die. Enjoy being in it; know that it is all around you.' This was wonderful news; there was no need to seek but there was a chance to enjoy the element in which it lived.

St Paul, when he was speaking about God to the Greeks on the Areopagus, says, 'In him we live and move and have our being' (Acts 17:28). This is a wonderful reality to discover: we need not seek God for we are in God, in his presence and in his love. Let us enjoy this reality.

33 The Good Shepherd

Aim

To show how much the Good Shepherd cares for us and will do for us.

Reading

John 10:1-18

Illustration

There was a group of shepherds who often talked about caring for their sheep. Yet, when trouble came, some did not want to bother; others said the sheep were not worth the risk; one or two took the money and left. One could be heard saying, 'You cannot believe a lamb is worth the life of a shepherd.' The reply from a hired man was, 'Of course it is not.'

Listening to all this was the good shepherd. It made him sad to think that the sheep were not truly loved. He loved his sheep dearly and would do anything to save them. Suddenly an old man came to him and said, 'I have been looking at your flock and you have a ewe lamb missing. She has wandered off and is in danger of death.' The shepherd left the comfort of home and the safety of his surroundings and began the search. Some were sure he should not have bothered. There were plenty of other sheep; why bother with a wayward one? The shepherd's life was more precious than the lamb's. The shepherd was soon travelling dark valleys. More than once he was at risk himself. Briars tore at his hands and his feet. There was a gaping hole in his side. Thorns had pierced his head. He was calling the lamb by name. At last there was a weak response. It was down a steep slope and in danger of falling further. The shepherd did not fear but descended into the depths. The darkness was trying to hold on to the lamb. The shepherd reached into the thorn bushes and became entangled; he was caught alongside the lamb. Even now he reached out to comfort it. There he lay, life ebbing out of him. He was trapped for more than 48 hours. But on the third day he broke free and rising up brought the lamb with him. He carried it all the way home. When they saw him they rejoiced. 'Just see how much he loves his flock and what he was willing to suffer for one little ewe lamb.'

34 Rescued from above

Aim

To rejoice in the presence of the ascended Lord.

Reading

Psalm 18:16-19

Illustration

At first there was a silence, as if we had been left to our own devices. Through our foolishness we had been caught by a rising tide. We had sent up a plea, by means of a telephone in the refuge box that was placed on stilts above the waves. Some caring people had built this place of comparative safety on the sands to accommodate fools who disobeyed the guidelines of safe crossings.

Suddenly there was a whirring sound from on high. It was no vision. It was a Sea King helicopter. A man was coming down from the safety of the helicopter and being lowered to where we were. He was very friendly. He did not tell us off. He did not say he came to admire the scenery! He said to each of us in turn, 'Do not worry. You will be all right. Fasten yourself to me.' Once one of us was fastened to him he signalled to the helicopter above and we were raised to safety. He came down four times altogether. He told us sometimes he was actually dropped into a raging sea to pick someone up. His purpose was always the same: he came down that we might be lifted up; he descended that we might ascend with him. Then we were taken to dry land. I looked back on my poor old car with water flowing almost over its roof. It would be a write-off. But we were safe. A little like the resurrection of the body and our being lifted to heaven. Words of Psalm 18:16-19 came to mind: 'He reached down from on high, he took me; he drew me out of mighty waters . . . He brought me out into a broad place: he delivered me because he delighted in me.'

Jesus came down that we might be raised up on high.

35 Sufficient energy

Aim

To rejoice in the presence and power of the Spirit.

Readings

Acts 1:8
Isaiah 40:31

Illustration

One of Europe's leading ecologists has said the energy crisis we face is not so much in energy supplies but in our own thinking. There is enough energy in the ebb and flow of the tides, in the running of rivers, in the winds and in the rays of the sun to supply our needs if we would give time and attention to these. Three things are obvious:

(1) Many energy supplies are limited and will run out.

(2) Wrong thinking or lack of proper attention makes us do nothing.

(3) All around there is power that we do not realise.

Too often the Church tries to go along in its own resources and strength, and it can be seen to be running out of supplies. We spend too much of our attention looking in the wrong direction.

The power of God is here, for the Lord is here: His Spirit is with us.

We need to learn to wait upon the Lord and the power of his might.

36 The power of the Lord

Aim

To learn to turn to Jesus in the storms of life.

Reading

Mark 4:35-41

Illustration

Do you know the story of Aladdin and his lamp? The lamp had wonderful powers but most people did not recognise it. The lamp standing unused was no better than any other. It could give out a little light but its great power remained untapped. It is no use having a wonderful power if you do not use it. In the same way, it is no use saying you believe in a Saviour if you do not call upon him.

Too often we allow Jesus to sleep in our lives. We struggle on alone and are often overwhelmed because we do not call upon him in the storm. While we allow fear to mount and energies to be overpowered, we fail to call upon the greatest power, which is our Lord.

In the storms of fear and sorrow, when we are feeling overwhelmed, we need to know the presence and the power of our God. We need to know again that God can bring order out of chaos and that Christ can give us his peace. Do not let Jesus sleep in your life; call upon him each day. Take heed these words from Julian of Norwich:

> He said not: 'Thou shalt not be tempest-tossed; thou shalt not be work-weary; thou shalt not be distressed.' But he did say: 'Thou shalt not be overcome.'

37 The gift of the kingdom

Aim

To compare the rule of Herod with the rule of Jesus.

Reading

Luke 12:32

Illustration

So many rulers rule by force. They often think of their subjects as objects for their own selfish ends. If people do not obey, there are ways of dealing with them, which include torture, imprisonment and even death. Dictators throughout history have got rid of those who opposed them by exterminating them; there are many tyrannical governments in our world that still operate like this.

The kingdom of heaven is the free gift of God's presence and love to us. It is not forced upon us but is offered freely. God loves us before we even turn to him. We are not rejected from his kingdom. We leave it of our own free will when we do not obey the King in love.

38 Seeking the lost

Aim

To show that we need times of quietness and rest.

Reading

Luke 15:4-7

Illustration

There was a famous General who met a poor shepherd. The shepherd was distressed because he had lost a lamb and could not find it. The General offered to help and sent his soldiers in search of the lamb. One by one the soldiers returned to camp hungry, muddied and feeling too tired to carry on. It was dark by then and they felt they could do nothing more. The next morning, just as it was getting light, the General was seen coming into the camp carrying the lamb under his greatcoat to keep it warm. This is what made him such a great leader: he was not put off and he did not think of himself too much. He only stopped looking for the lamb when he found it. (You can compare this to the Good Shepherd.)

39 Shining in the dark

Aim

To seek to abide in Jesus and let him abide in us.

Readings

2 Corinthians 4:6
Ephesians 5:8

Illustration

There was once a man who bought a beautiful box for his wife. The box had flowers on the top and they would glow in the dark. As it was for her birthday he hid it away in a drawer and left it there for a few weeks. On her birthday it was given to her all wrapped in a lovely parcel. She was delighted and could hardly wait until the evening. When it got dark she looked at the box but it did not shine; it had not changed at all. They both waited until it got really dark but the box never did shine. They felt a little cheated because the box was bought to shine. Then a little note fell from the packaging. It said, 'If you want me to shine all night, you need put me in the sun all day.' The box would only glow if it was left out in the daylight. They left it out all the next day and, true to the words, all night it glowed with a splendid light.

If we are to glow with eternal life, we need to be placed in the presence of the Son of God to let him abide in us and for us to know we abide in him.

40 A faithful helper

Aim

To affirm our commitment to Christ.

Readings

Deuteronomy 31:6
John 14:18

Illustration

Here is a story of loyalty. A man and his dog walked in the hill country. The man saw an old mine in a hillside and went in. Whilst inside, the roof collapsed and trapped the man by his leg. For a while the dog stayed with him but it then went outside the mine and stood at the entrance. There it began to howl to attract attention. No one took any notice at first. The dog became hungry and thirsty but it did not leave its post. The weather became bad; the dog got wet and cold but it stayed put and continued to howl. Finally a nearby farmer decided there was something wrong with the dog and he climbed the hillside to find it. When he arrived, the dog stopped howling but would not let him touch it or even feed it. It tried to lead him into the mine. The farmer made to go away but as soon as he did this the dog started to howl and to walk towards the mine again. At last he decided to go to the entrance and call to see if there was anyone there. He heard a voice and so went cautiously inside. He saw the man was trapped and went for help. The dog seemed to understand because it now stayed with its master and remained with him until help came and he was rescued.

41 Unity

Aim

To express the unity of all believers, as there is only 'One Church, one faith, one Lord'.

Readings

Genesis 18:1-15
Hebrews 13:2

Illustration

Hospitality was of great importance in the ancient world. By being open to others, the great Other, who is God, was given the opportunity to enter into your life. See the example of Abraham and Sarah when visited by the Lord (Genesis 18:1-15). In the story it is hard to decide whether we are dealing with three men, three angels or the three-person God. Ask the congregation who visited Abraham: was it men, angels, God? (Be careful how you phrase the question for it is not an 'either/or'. All visited Abraham at Mamre. The person that replies 'Yes' to the question or says, 'All three' would get top marks!)

There is a Celtic poem which expresses the Other approaching us through others.

> I saw a stranger yestere'en
> I put food in the eating place,
> drink in the drinking place,
> music in the listening place
> and in the sacred name of the Triune
> he blessed myself and my house,
> my cattle and my dear ones,
> and the lark said in her song
> often, often, often,
> goes the Christ in a stranger's guise.

42 Under control

Aim

To show that Christ is King and seeks to rule in our hearts.

Readings

Matthew 24:7-14
Romans 8:18-23, 35-39

Illustration

The school bus is at the top of a steep hill when the driver slumps at the wheel. The bus starts to swerve all over the road and is picking up speed. There is general panic on the bus for it is out of control. Two lads rush forward and move the driver off the seat. A girl grabs the steering wheel and gently applies the brakes. She has never driven before but knows what to do. One minute everything was out of control and the next the busload of children was rescued by the quick thinking and acting of three young people.

The world seems to have a tendency to run out of control; wars and rumours of wars, famine and earthquakes, violence and force seem to take over. Jesus warned us that these things would happen but that we should see them as the birth pangs of the new age, the coming of God's kingdom. We should celebrate that God is in control, that Christ is our Redeemer and King.

43 God waiting and watching

Aim

To show how God delights in all who turn to him.

Reading

Luke 15:1-10

Illustration

A letter from God

When you awoke, I was there, waiting upon you. I wanted to share in your love.

At breakfast you listened to the radio and rushed your breakfast. You had no time to speak to me. I waited but you did not turn to me.

Though you travelled by rail you spent your time on your laptop and reading the news. You did not once give me a thought. And I waited for you to turn to me.

During your work there were lots of small gaps. There was more time at lunch. But you did other things and had no time for me. Yet I waited for you to turn to me.

At the end of the day you watched the television and played a game. For a while you dozed before you had your last drink of the day. And I waited for you to turn to me.

Now, I thought, you will have time – just before you go to sleep. Instead, you read until you were tired. You worried about tomorrow and at last fell asleep.

I will surround you with my love this night. I will wait for you tomorrow and if you do not remember I will be there the day after. I will wait until you turn to me.

All my love, God.

44 Letting God in

Aim

To encourage people to trust in God and to invite him into their daily life.

Reading

Luke 12:32-40

Illustration

Look at Holman Hunt's painting 'Light of the World'. Here Christ is at a door knocking. The lack of a handle on the outside of the door shows it can only be opened from within. The weeds around the door show that it has not been opened for a long time. The apples lying on the ground remind us of the fall from grace in the Garden of Eden. Through sin, people and God become separate. Jesus comes to unite us again with God if we will let him into our lives.

45 The peace of Christ's presence

Aim

To show that Christ offers us his peace and his presence.

Reading

John 14:23-29

Illustration

In the old days crossing the Atlantic in a sailing boat left everyone to the mercy of the wind and waves. How those old wooden boats rocked about! People not used to the rolling of the boat could not walk on deck. Many had to spend most of their voyage below deck. Everything that could be was fastened firmly down to prevent it from being washed overboard. Today's journeys are a great contrast. Waiters can carry soup and children can play on deck. People lounge in the sun and hardly notice the rising and falling of the waves. Even in a storm the main body of the ship remains relatively calm – all because of the unseen gyroscope that maintains the balance of the ship. We have been offered the power of peace and calm in our lives through the presence of Christ. Do we accept this offer or neglect it at our peril?

46 God in us

Aim

To rejoice that we dwell in God and he in us.

Reading

John 17:20-26

Illustration

There is an old story about God and the humans after the Fall. Because man had separated from God through disobedience, God decided to hide from humans. He asked his angels where he should hide. 'Hide in the heights of heaven,' said the first angel. God replied, 'The humans would expect me to be in the high places and they will find me in their own high experiences.' The second angel said, 'Then why not hide in the depths?' God replied, 'Again, all human beings descend into the depths from time to time and they will discover that I am there.' One little angel had bided his time and he saw the mistakes of others. He said to God, 'Why not hide in the human heart? They will never find you there.' God smiled and said, 'How true', and from that day hid in each human heart. Yet there are so few humans who seek his presence in their lives.

47 Who is my neighbour?

Aim

To explore the question 'Who is my neighbour?'

Reading

Luke 10:25-37

Illustration

There is a story about Martin, a cobbler. He looked forward to the coming of the Lord and felt he would soon come to visit his shop. He busied himself getting ready, but he was often interrupted. He saw a child getting into trouble in the market place, so he went out to help him. Then he saw a poor woman who was in need of better shoes. He called her into the shop and saw to her needs. After this there was an old man who looked frozen. He invited the man in and gave him a warm drink. Martin would have liked to have prepared more for the coming of the Lord but he ran out of time. Martin reached out to all who came his way. That night Martin had a dream in which he saw the Lord. The Lord told him how he had visited him when the child needed help, when the woman needed shoes and when the old man wanted some warmth. In caring for his neighbour, Martin met the Lord.

48 Meeting us where we are

Aim

To know that Jesus comes to where we are and seeks to help us to rise with him.

Reading

Luke 19:1-10

Illustration

John was put in prison for the third time. He had a good mind but he used it for crime. He was a robber and occasionally given to violence. Even his family had given up on him. He rarely had any visitors other than the official prison visitors. One day he asked the man who had been coming to see him regularly why he bothered. The man explained he believed that everyone was important and could change, even John. He also told him that he was a Christian and so believed everyone was precious in the eyes of God. This really made John think: a God that actually knew him and loved him, that he need not be condemned for ever. John began to read the Gospels and the story of Jesus. He said he had never felt such a love or known forgiveness up to that time. John became a changed man. When he was released from prison he got work with an aid agency through the help of his prison visitor. He became a trusted and hard worker and in time held a position of great trust. He never hesitated to explain how he had plumbed the depths and how Jesus had reached down to him.

49 God in the here and now

Aim

To show how Jesus begins his ministry through the Church and the Scriptures.

Reading

Luke 4:14-21

Illustration

There is the story of a Celtic monk who decided to give up study and only to pray. His abbess asked how his mind would be fed if he gave up study. The monk persisted and said that he would leave where he was and go and search for God overseas. The abbess replied, 'If God cannot be found on this side of the sea, by all means let us journey overseas. But since God is near all those who call on him, we have no need to cross the sea. The kingdom of God can be reached from every land.'

There is a great need for us to know that God is with us today and God desires to bring in his kingdom through us today. Psalm 95 need always be heeded: 'O that today you would listen to his voice!' (verse 7).

50 Immersed in God

Aim

To affirm our belief in the Holy Trinity and in the mission of Christ.

Reading

Luke 3:15-17, 21, 22

Illustration

There is a species of water fly which flies in the air but dives into the water for its food. It can survive in the water because, as it dives, it takes an air bubble with it. It moves around inside the air bubble until it gets what it wants and then returns to the air. It survives in the water because it is surrounded by air.

Our God surrounds us; we are immersed in his presence. St Paul tells us this when he says 'In him we live and move and have our being' (Acts 17:28). In baptism, our being immersed in water is an outward sign of our total immersion in the presence and power of God.

51 A transforming presence

Aim

To show that the presence of Jesus transforms our lives.

Reading

John 2:1-11

Illustration

The car was running well, there was nothing wrong with the engine or the electrics but it suddenly came to a halt. It had juddered for a while and then came to a standstill. There was no way it would start again for it had run out of fuel.

The driver had to sit there on a lonely country road hoping for help. Fortunately there came a farmer on a tractor and he offered to give the car a tow. The driver was not keen as this was quite a new car. When the farmer looked he realised the car had run out of petrol. He had a full can on the farm, so he went away but soon returned and poured the petrol into the tank. He gave the petrol to the driver as a gift and said as he saw him off, 'None of us can run on an empty tank.'

There are times in life when our human resources run out. Then the harder we try, the worse it gets. There are many people who are drained or running near empty; now and again we all need our batteries recharged.

Listen to these words: 'Those who wait for the Lord shall renew their strength' (Isaiah 40:31); or these words of Jesus: 'Come to me, all you who are weary and are carrying heavy burdens, and I will give you rest' (Matthew 11:28).

52 Seek and find

Aim

To show we are all seekers and need to come to the Christ.

Reading

Matthew 2:1-12

Illustration

(This can be said by three different people.)

I bring gold because I am a rich man. I have all sorts of wonderful possessions and I have a good mind. I really am well off. I can buy whatever I want. But there are some things money cannot buy. You cannot buy love or health; you cannot buy peace of mind or eternal life. I offer gold to the One who can give me what money cannot buy.

I bring frankincense, the precious gum of a tree. Incense is used in worship. I am well-off, with a good mind. But it is easy to feel self-sufficient or over-important. I need to look beyond myself, to look at the mysteries and wonders of life. I need to know God to be satisfied. In adoration I offer incense to the One who meets my needs and tells me God is here.

I bring myrrh that relieves pain, for I have tasted many sufferings. I am a clever man but I cannot escape pain or the fear of death. I offer myrrh for all the sorrowful people of the world, for all who are heavily burdened, for all whose labour is hard. I offer myrrh for all who are in pain or distress, to the One who tells us that God cares. God will give us freedom. God will relieve our pain. God will give us life eternal.

Together:
We offer our gifts to God who gives himself to us.

53 Raising us up to God

Aim

To rejoice in the presence of the ascended Lord.

Reading

Luke 24:44-53

Illustration

A man was wandering carelessly without looking where he was going. The result was he fell into a well. The well was deep and dark, and the dirt and slime clung to the man. He knew that he could perish in this horrible place.

The God of the Old Testament, the God of the Law, came and said, 'If you had kept to the right path, you would not have ended up like this. You have strayed from the straight and narrow and now you are suffering for it. One day you will be given a rescuer.'

Allah then came and looked down at the man and said, 'It is the will of Allah. Fate has brought you here. You could not escape from this whatever you did. But it may be my will that you get out again.'

Buddha looked down on the man and said, 'Smile, for it is all in the mind. Cleanse your mind and everything will be all right.'

Jesus said nothing. He descended into the mud and mire. He experienced the dark, the pain, the discomfort. He was there in the depths taking hold of the man. Then, through great efforts that cost him dearly, Jesus rose and when he ascended he took the man with him.

54 Ready and waiting

Aim

To look at the Benedictus and to rejoice in our saving God.

Reading

Luke 1:68-79

Illustration

In the time of Jesus, when a king was about to make a journey a messenger was sent out before him. Each area would be told the king was coming. This was so that they could prepare properly. They would fill in any holes in the road and level off any awkward bumps so that the king's journey would be smooth and without hindrance.

The other task of the messenger was to make sure that people prepared themselves properly, and if the king was coming to stay, there would be room for him and that the people would give him attention.

John the Baptist was to prepare the way for Jesus, so that the people would be ready to accept him.

55 Extraordinarily ordinary

Aim

To celebrate the coming of the Saviour into the world.

Reading

Luke 2:1-14

Illustration

There was a Scottish farmer who refused to believe the Christmas story. Though his wife and children went to church, he refused to and often mocked them. Why should God lower himself to be like us? It is foolish talk.

Once when it was snowing, the family went to church. The farmer noticed that the snow was getting much worse. Suddenly he heard a thump against his window and then another. He went out to see what was happening. There in front of him was a large flock of geese which had got lost in the storm.

The farmer was kind and felt for them. He wanted to help them. He realised that they could shelter in his barn. He got behind them and tried to drive them in, but they only scattered. Then he tried by laying a trail of food to the barn door, but the geese did not take any notice. There was nothing he could do to get them to enter the barn.

About to give up on them he said to himself, 'Why don't they follow me? If I were a goose, I could lead them into the barn. If I looked like one of them, I could save them.'

Suddenly he stopped and thought about what he had said: he could only save them by becoming like them. Suddenly he understood the great love of God for humankind. He fell to his knees in the snow and gave thanks to God for his great love.

56 Jesus the Anointed One

Aim

To rejoice in the sacrificial love of Mary, which is a foretaste of the sacrifice of Christ the 'Anointed One'.

Reading

John 12:1-8

Illustration

A nurse in hospital described how humans have a great capacity for accepting what is happening to them and for enduring pain as long as they have loved ones about them and people who truly care. Pain can be borne as long as we are not left alone. We need to know in our troubles that we are still loved and cared for. Worse than pain is the feeling of separation from loved ones or a feeling that we are no longer wanted.

When many were beginning to go against Jesus – including Judas – it is good to see the expression of love and affection that is shown him from the whole household at Bethany.

57 Faith in his presence

Aim

To share in the joy of Easter.

Reading

John 20:19-31

Illustration

As a young man, before he became Archbishop, Anthony Bloom was an atheist; but he was a seeker. He heard a lecture on Jesus and just could not believe what he heard. He picked up a Bible and turned to the Gospels. He counted the chapters of each Gospel so that he could read the shortest. He chose St Mark and this is what he said:

> I started to read St Mark's Gospel . . . before I reached the third chapter, I suddenly became aware that on the other side of my desk there was a presence. And the certainty was so strong that it was the Christ standing there that it has never left me. This was the real turning point. Because Christ was alive and I had been in his presence.

Prayer

58 Listening

Aim

To learn the value of listening.

Reading

1 Samuel 3:9

Illustration

Hello!
Are you receiving me?
Hello!
Are you receiving me?
Hello!
Are you receiving me?

This was a conversation, if you can call it that, on a mobile phone. The person was in a bad reception area. There was too much interference from hills and trees. They would have to go to a better reception area.

It is amazing how many people and nations are good at speaking but find it very hard to hear anyone. Our speakers (mouths) seem to be far more active than our receivers (ears). A proverb from the East says, 'God gave us two ears and one mouth so that we should listen twice as much as we speak.'

59 Charging our batteries

Aim

To show the need for prayer.

Reading

Isaiah 40:31

Illustration

It is not often you see one of these in church – a battery charger. Sometimes, even when there is fuel in the tank, the engine will not start. This is because there is no spark, no electricity to fire the engine. Then you need the battery charger. It will slowly revive the flat battery and give it new life. Then we will be able to get going again. Also a car cannot run for long without being refuelled. You need to fill it up regularly with petrol. The more miles you do, the more petrol you need.

Some of you may have battery chargers at home to charge up batteries for CD players or other things that need electricity to keep them going. Many modern torches come with a charger so that the battery can produce a bright light.

Sometimes people are a bit like a beautiful car with a full tank of petrol but a flat battery. They should be able to do all sorts but they are flat and dull or feeling run down. So many seem to lack a bright spark in their lives. When this is so, we need power from outside ourselves. Listen again to Isaiah: 'Those who wait for the Lord shall renew their strength.'

60 Contact

Aim

To show Jesus is the giver of hope and life.

Reading

Mark 5:30

Illustration

How often do we lose contact with friends because we do not make the effort? To maintain a relationship with anyone we need to meet them and talk to them. If they are far away we can at least write, telephone or send an e-mail. A once-a-year Christmas card could hardly be called contact.

In a car the contacts give a vital spark that fires the engine. If the contacts are broken, the engine will not fire properly. Even if we have plenty of fuel and the battery is charged, the car will not go if there are no contacts at work.

When Jesus asks, 'Who touched me?' could you say, 'It was I, Lord'? Do you keep in proper contact with Jesus? When the woman touched him, power travelled from Jesus to her. We so often fail to achieve because we go it alone and do not touch base with Jesus.

(You might like to use the hymn 'What a friend we have in Jesus'; let the people read it during a silence.)

61 Prayer and hypocrisy

Aim

To make sure our traditions do not hinder our relationship with God.

Reading

Matthew 6:5-6

Illustration

A devout Muslim carries his prayer mat around with him and prays a fixed number of times each day. At the fixed times he will unroll his mat and turn to God. This is a wonderful way of keeping in contact with his creator.

There was a certain Muslim who had great anger in his heart. He was in hot pursuit of a man whom he wanted to kill. He had a dagger and was intent on murder. Suddenly the call to prayer rang out from the mosque. The man stopped for a moment, rushed his prayers, then continued on his murderous chase. The prayer was part of his daily ritual but he did not let it touch his heart. This man could be seen to be a hypocrite.

62 True love

Aim

To encourage love of God and of each other.

Reading

Matthew 22:36-39; 19:21-22

Illustration

My Dearest,

I love you with all my heart.

I think of you every minute of the day.

I would do anything for you. I would swim shark-infested rivers to get to you. I would climb the steepest of mountains. I would travel the whole earth to be with you. I would brave fire and frost, wind and hail to be at your side.

But I cannot see you this week. I was coming tonight but it is too cold and damp for me to bother. Tomorrow I have fitness training and I am out with the lads the day after. I have a new computer game I want to try out on Wednesday, and a match to go to on Thursday. Friday as ever is swimming, and on Saturday the finals are on the television. I would do anything for you but it is a busy week. Sorry.

Keep in touch,

Yours always.

Not what I would call a promising relationship but is this the way we often deal with God and our prayers? Do we really love the Lord with all our heart?

63 Make room for Jesus

Aim

To understand that we need to make room for Jesus in our lives.

Reading

John 1:1-14

Illustration

Nan-in was a great Japanese teacher of the art of Zen. One day a university professor came to seek some teaching. Nan-in served the traditional tea to his guest. He poured until his visitor's bowl was full and then kept pouring and the tea overflowed, as there was no room for it in the bowl. The professor watched until he could no longer restrain himself and said, 'It is overfull and no more will go in.' Nan-in said, 'You are like this cup. You are full of ideas and speculations. How can I pour more in unless you empty your cup? You need to make space to learn.'

In the same way we need to make a space in our lives each day for our God who comes to us.

Think upon these words by Angelus Silesius:

Though Christ a thousand times
in Bethlehem be born,
if he is not born in you,
you are still forlorn.

64 Attentiveness

Aim

To show the need for stillness and to be receptive to our God.

Reading

Luke 10:38-42

Illustration

The greatest danger of television is that it encourages us to switch off from one another. This is true of iPods and personal CD players. They all help to shut us off and enclose us in a world of our own. But we do not need any of these to be inattentive. A child comes in with an important message but the father is filling in his tax forms and the mother is busy preparing the dinner. 'But . . .' says the child and is still not given attention. The parents have not listened and the child is left feeling alone. The generation gap is often created because we do not listen to each other. The child goes out and wonders who will look at the washing machine that is overflowing!

65 Perseverance

Aim
To show that we need to persevere in our prayers.

Reading
Luke 18:1-8

Illustration
St Teresa of Avila showed a great enthusiasm for life. In the front of her prayer book these words were written:

> Let nothing disturb thee,
> nothing affright thee,
> all things are passing,
> God never changes.
> Patient endurance
> attaineth to all things.
> Who God possesses
> in nothing is wanting.
> God alone suffices.

These are deep words indeed and should be thought about with care. (Make copies available – as a bookmark – to all who would like to think about the words.)

66 The experience of grace

Aim

To make God the centre of our prayers and to rejoice in his grace and goodness.

Reading

Luke 18:9-14

Illustration

The outside of the house looked well in the twilight. The white-washed walls seemed to shine and even more so in the moonlight. Then during the night it snowed and we awoke to a bright morning. How shabby the outside of the house looked against the brightness of the snow and the sunlight – it certainly needed a coat of paint. How we are depends on what or whom we compare ourselves with. When we are placed before the grace and holiness of God, all that we can truly say is 'God, be merciful to me, a sinner.'

67 Exploring the Lord's prayer

Aim

To explore the Lord's Prayer.

Reading

Luke 11:1-13

Illustration

When we turn to God in prayer we acknowledge his presence: that God is with us always and that he listens to us. You are actually in the presence, in God. We are in God in the same way as fish live in water and we in air. Listen to these words by the poet Francis Thompson from the poem 'No Strange Land':

> Does the fish soar to find the ocean,
> the eagle plunge to find the air –
> that we ask of the stars in motion
> if they have rumour of thee there?

We cannot search for God but we can open ourselves to his presence, and a good way of doing this is by speaking to him quietly each day.

Use the Lord's Prayer and pause between each phrase to be ware of the fullness and wonder of the words and of your God.

68 Tuned in to God

Aim

To continue to rejoice in the Word made flesh.

Reading

John 1:1-18

Illustration

Some people live in poor reception areas for television or radio. The signal cannot get to them so the picture or the sound is blurred, fuzzy and cannot be enjoyed properly. Many things can cause bad reception. People can live too far from the transmitter. Sometimes it is just that their aerial is pointing the wrong way and it needs to be turned around. Are you sure you are pointing in the right direction? At other times it is something close that destroys reception – a motor without a suppressor, or a lot of leaves on nearby trees that can block the signal. Then again it can be the opposite: there is too much interference because the set is too receptive. All sorts of sounds distort what we need to hear. We need to be able to finely tune to make proper contact. This is as true of prayer as it is of radio waves.

69 Seeking the way

Aim

To encourage people not to 'suppose' the presence of Jesus but to seek to know he is with us.

Reading

Luke 2:41-52

Illustration

There are so many ways that people can get lost. There is a lovely story of an absent-minded professor from Edinburgh. He used to travel regularly by train and all the ticket collectors knew him. Once by the gate he was anxiously going through his pockets and after a while the ticket collector asked if he could help. 'I have lost my ticket,' said the professor. 'That's all right, sir, we all know you. You can get on the train.' 'But,' said the professor, 'I need my ticket because I do not know where I am going.'

It is easy to get lost in this world. Do you know where you are going?

70 The power and guidance of the Spirit

Aim

To know the Spirit as our strength and our guide.

Reading

Acts 2:1-21

Illustration

There are lots of ancient stories about werewolves and creatures that come in the night and steal away your life powers. You wake in the morning feeling drained and half-dead. Well, you might not believe such tales but it is still possible to awake short on energy and resources, and the more we try to put it right, the more in danger we are of becoming exhausted. When our batteries run low we need a charge from outside of ourselves. Too many of us think we are self-sufficient, able to go in our own strength, when we need to learn to wait upon the Lord for renewal and for guidance. Just as we would not drive around all day with a flat tyre, so we should make sure we begin the day filled with the power and love of God.

Love, wealth and happiness

71 Abusing the rules

Aim

To show that lives are richer than the keeping of rules – but that rules are necessary.

Reading

Matthew 5:19; 23:23-24

Illustration

Rules and regulations are there to help us and the society we live in. Occasionally you hear of some absurd application of the law, usually by someone who says something like, 'It's more than my job's worth.' A young motorcyclist was knocked off his bike in an area of parking meters. His bike was put carefully at the side of the road. Even though the traffic warden knew of the event, he placed a parking ticket on the bike. Fortunately, the city council was more understanding when a plea was made. Some people find it very hard to understand that rules are there to help us rather than hinder us.

72 Unheeded warning

Aim

To show that our relationships are important.

Reading

Psalm 8

Illustration

Once a bird flying high overhead saw how our world was becoming polluted. The bird saw the rubbish dumped into the sea and fish struggling to survive, great tracts of land being robbed of trees, the ice-caps slowly melting. So it decided that it must tell the humans about what was happening. The first group would not listen – well, who would believe a bird! The next group were making good profits and did not want anything to be disturbed. A third group said they would happily talk about it for years. No one wanted to do anything. Yet the bird knew that all things were linked together. If the humans destroyed the environment, all the birds and all the animals would also suffer. Why were the humans so insensitive to their surroundings and to each other? The bird learnt that the humans had lost a sense of awe and wonder because they had broken their relationship with the Creator God. If they would not listen to the cries of creation, if they would not listen to the voice of God, they were not likely to hear a bird.

73 The blind leading the blind

Aim

To show that Jesus opens our eyes to the reality of the world.

Reading

Luke 6:39

Illustration

The comic character Mr Magoo is funny because he is short-sighted, though in real life he would be a tragic person. He walks across crocodiles thinking they are logs. He steps out of a window in high-rise flats just as a window cleaner's hoist reaches the window. He steps off the side of a pier as a boat pulls level alongside. He does not come to harm but he often leaves a trail of chaos and disaster behind him.

Can we see what is happening around us, to our communities and the way we are shaping the future? Or are we content to leave it in the hands of those who are blind to many of the finer things of life? If we allow the blind to lead us, will we not both fall into the ditch?

It is of extreme importance that we make sure we are led by men and women of vision. It is no use having a quick fix or a laugh now if we are destroying our future. Pray for vision for yourself and your leaders.

74 Opportunity

Aim

To show that God calls each of us and we all have an opportunity to answer that call.

Reading

Mark 1:16-20

Illustration

The need to react to God's call is caught well in Shakespeare's *Julius Caesar*, Act IV:

> There is a tide in the affairs of men,
> Which, taken at the flood leads on to fortune;
> Omitted, all the voyage of their life
> Is bound in shallows and in miseries.
> On such a full sea we are now afloat,
> And we must take the current when it serves,
> Or lose our ventures.

Fortunately, our God will call us again and again. There is a time when we have to stop talking about Christ and set out to follow him.

Jesus calls us, whoever we are.

There was once a very ordinary man (if there is such a being) called Aeshines, who came to Socrates and said, 'I am a poor man. I have nothing to give you but myself.' Socrates replied, 'Do you not see that you are giving me the most precious thing of all?'

Jesus wants the gift of ourselves far more than talk and theory. Will we truly seek to follow him?

75 Love one another

Aim

To show that Jesus makes all the difference.

Readings

Matthew 3:13-17
1 John 4:7-21

Illustration

What a difference Jesus makes. *Miracle on the River Kwai* by Ernest Gordon tells the story of prisoners of war building a bridge. They were overworked, often starving, exhausted and ill. The need to survive made them put themselves first and fail to see each other's needs. Then two men, Dusty and Dinty, began helping others. They put themselves out to care for and respect others. A new spirit began to spread through the camp until the place was transformed, as were its inhabitants. When questioned about their actions, Dusty read from 1 John 4:21: 'The commandment we have from him is this: those who love God must love their brothers and sisters also.' Dusty was a Methodist and Dinty a Roman Catholic, and both were full of the Presence. The lives of the men had been hell. Then 'Jesus came' and what a difference that made.

76 Jesus fills our emptiness

Aim

To show how Jesus fills our emptiness and our longing for God.

Reading

John 4:5-42

Illustration

Bill had tried everything to fill the gnawing emptiness that he felt inside. Whenever there was a time of quiet, the feeling of emptiness and worthlessness came upon him. He sought to escape into never having silence. Music, videos, computer games filled up his emptiness – but he knew it was still there. He tried to escape in thrills, in excitement, in sex and drugs. But underneath, the gnawing feeling was there. He felt alone and empty. One day, listening to the radio, Bill heard a poem by Francis Thompson called 'The Hound of Heaven'. The whole poem seemed to be about him. Certain lines, he said, struck home, especially these:

> 'All things betray thee, who betrayest me.'
>
> 'Naught shelters thee, who will not shelter me.'

And later:

> 'Lo! Naught contents thee, who content'st not me.'

He realised his emptiness was because he had been on the run from God. In tears, this big strong man committed himself to God in prayer. He started going to church and became a much more fulfilled and contented person. He came to love the Psalms and in particular Psalms 42 and 43.

77 Hospitality

Aim

To show how through hospitality Christ can be proclaimed and accepted.

Reading

Matthew 10:40-42

Illustration

The Selfish Giant banned the children from his garden. He built a wall around it and put up a notice saying:

TRESPASSERS
WILL BE
PROSECUTED

From that time spring did not come to the giant's garden and it remained winter. By keeping himself to himself, there was no warmth in the place.

Only when the children sneaked back did spring return with them. It was then that the giant realised his hostility to the children had kept him in the cold.

(Read the full story of the Selfish Giant in *The Happy Prince* by Oscar Wilde, Puffin Books.)

Hostility brings about isolation. Hospitality opens us to the warmth of relationships.

78 Enough for all

Aim

To show that the compassion of Jesus can reach out to others through our willingness to give and share.

Reading

Matthew 14:13-21

Illustration

This is the story of the 'long spoons'. Someone was given a vision of what life is like. She went into a room where there was a lot of food to be eaten but only by a long spoon. The spoon was so long that the people could not get it to their mouths and food was being spilled and wasted. Everyone looked frustrated and hungry. It looked like a picture of hell.

Then she went into another room where there were still long spoons and the same system. Here everyone was feeding someone else. They were reaching out and feeding a neighbour. Here there was much laughter and fellowship. It felt more like heaven than hell.

She thought long on this and realised that there is enough in the world for everyone's need but not for their greed.

79 Forgiveness rebuilds relationships

Aim

To show that we should seek forgiveness and the rebuilding of relationships.

Reading

Matthew 18:15-20

Illustration

In the story *Great Expectations* by Charles Dickens, Pip has dealt badly with Joe the blacksmith who cared for him in his early days. When Pip was ill and in debt, Joe came to care for him. Joe stayed by him, gave him cooling drinks.

> At last, one day, I took courage, and said, 'Is it Joe?'
>
> And the dear old home-voice answered, 'Which it air, old chap.'
>
> 'Oh Joe, you break my heart! Look angry at me, Joe! Strike me, Joe! Tell me of my ingratitude. Don't be so good to me.'
>
> For Joe had actually laid his head down on the pillow at my side and put his arm around my neck, in his joy that I knew him.
>
> 'Which dear old Pip, old chap,' said Joe, 'you and me was ever friends. And when you are well enough to go out for a ride – what larks!'
>
> After which Joe withdrew to the window and stood with his back towards me, wiping his eyes. And as my extreme weakness prevented me going to him, I lay there penitently whispering, 'O God bless him! God bless this gentle Christian man!'

80 The Beatitudes

Aim

To show that blessedness comes from God.

Reading

Matthew 5:1-12

Illustration

The word 'blessed' comes from the Greek word 'makarios' and is used to describe the gods. Jesus uses it to describe those who do God's will. The Greeks called Cyprus the 'blessed island' or the 'happy island' because it was such a rich and fertile land with a good climate, rich in minerals and natural resources. Fruit and grain and flowers could grow in abundance. It was a place where people should be perfectly happy. It should be a place of peace and harmony. In the same way, those who lived the beatitudes would find peace and harmony in God's presence and God's love.

81 Priorities

Aim

To see where our priorities lie and how we give our time to God.

Reading

Luke 16:1-13

Illustration

Richard became a junior in the sales department of a large firm when he left school. It was soon discovered he had a flair for sales. In time he became chief salesman, and at that stage he negotiated a percentage of each sale for himself. He was becoming well-off. He had a wonderful home, two expensive cars and a good deal of shares in the business. He was made head of the sales department and then a member of the board. All was wonderful and he was rich indeed. Yet something told him all was not right. One night, returning from a sales conference, he was involved in a serious accident and nearly lost his life. Whilst unconscious he said he was aware of some being in white saying, 'Pity he has not done so well in the things that matter. This man is still a child in spiritual things.' When he recovered he went back to work for a while. His 'visitation' bothered him. He started going to church with his wife and realised he had a lot to learn and that he was poor in spirit. But he gave himself to this as he did to his work. After a year he offered himself to train for the ministry. He was ordained and after two curacies, moved to Africa with his wife and family where they worked for a relief agency. When asked about his wealth, most of which he had given away, he would reply, 'I was never as rich as I am now.'

82 Treasuring humanity

Aim

To encourage a greater sensitivity towards each other and to the poor.

Reading

Luke 16:19-31

Illustration

I know a planet where there is a certain red-faced man. He has never smelled a flower; he has never looked at a star. He has never loved anyone. He never does anything in his life but add up figures. And all day long he says over and over, just like you, 'I am busy with matters of consequence,' and that makes him swell with pride. But he is not a man; he is a mushroom!

A what?

A mushroom.

(From *The Little Prince* by Antoine de Saint-Exupéry.)

His insensitivity made the man less than human.

83 Finding true wealth

Aim

To encourage an attitude of gratitude and to make people aware of the needs of lepers.

Reading

Luke 17:11-19

Illustration

Richard was diagnosed as having a serious cancer. He had a brain tumour and if nothing was done, he would die. He was a rich and powerful man and also a man of prayer. The first thing his illness did was make him appreciate all that he had and what was precious to him. Amid the fear of what lay ahead a new joy had entered his life and his home. Each time he went for treatment he committed himself not only to the hospital team but also to the love of God. He was sure, whatever the outcome, he would not be separated from God and his care. Richard was fortunate and he was cured and given a good few years to live. He never ceased to show his appreciation for life and all that was around him. He gave thanks to God each day for all he was able to do. On top of this he gave a proportion of his income each week to Cancer Research in thanksgiving for what had been done for him.

84 Happiness in giving

Aim

To look at the relationships we have with our possessions.

Reading

Luke 12:13-21

Illustration

When John Wesley was at Oxford he lived by a rule that he set himself: 'Save what you can and give away what you can.' At first Wesley had an income of £30 a year. He then lived off £28 and gave £2 away each year. When his income rose to £60 a year he lived on £28 and gave away £32. As his income rose to £60 and then to £120 a year, he still lived on £28 and gave the rest away.

The Accountant General for Household Plate (a sort of tax collector) asked for a return from Wesley supposing he should have a good deal to show. Wesley replied, 'I have two silver teaspoons at London and two at Bristol. This is all the plate which I have at present; and will not buy any more, while so many people around me want bread.'

85 Inner peace and happiness

Aim

To show that God is our key to happiness.

Reading

Luke 6:17-26

Illustration

It is amazing how many products offer us more happiness, when in fact they are only seeking to fulfil our consuming passion to have more. The notice of 'Happy Hour' at some places is always amusing, for if that is the 'happy hour', what is the rest of the time?

There are many stories of people who have sold their heart or their soul to make money. At first it is wonderful, for money can buy all sorts of things. But possessions alone cannot fill our inner emptiness; we also need love and to know we are of some value. There is nothing worse than the person that has made it in the world but is poor in the sight of his neighbours or God. There is a very telling story from Matthew 19:16-22: the rich young man sought eternal life (did he think he could buy it?) but 'he went away grieving, for he had many possessions' (verse 22).

86 Something money can't buy

Aim

To show that Christ is our peace among the storms of life.

Reading

Luke 8:22-25

Illustration

There was a man who, for some reason, raged against life. Because he did not start off with riches, he was angry with all rich people. He did not make friends easily and often got into trouble by his aggressive attitude. Everything he gained he kept to himself. Soon he was well-off and successful – but not happy. It seemed storms followed him around. He was not comfortable to be with. He was also very lonely. Then he became ill and he began to struggle; he needed the care and attention of someone. He could afford it and hired a group of carers. One was a nurse who was willing put herself out to help him. She did errands and stayed with him for company. She also told him that she gained great peace of mind from knowing Jesus. The man was embarrassed at first but then wanted to know more. He wanted to know why she cared for him and how Jesus brought peace. In time, as his health improved, he no longer needed carers but he felt he needed this nurse; in fact, he loved her and proposed to her. She accepted him, they married and lived very happily together. He also had a living relationship with Jesus and so he knew of love and peace in his life.

87 The Midas touch

Aim

To look at the song of Mary – the Magnificat.

Reading

Luke 1:39-55

Illustration

Love matters more than riches. This is well illustrated by the story of King Midas. In his greed he accepted the offer that all he touched would turn to gold. Very exciting! He touched plates, leaves, statues and they all turned to gold. He would soon be the richest man in the world. But his food also turned to gold and he began to starve. He touched his daughter and she turned to gold and he lost her warmth and her love. He had sold himself for riches and now he was poor indeed. He had all the gold you could dream about but he was poor within. Fortunately, this condition was reversible. Midas could lose the desire for gold and become loving and happy once more. When asked if he would like this rather than gold his reply was 'Yes'.

Signs of glory

88 Filling a vacuum

Aim

To encourage people to think about the Holy Trinity.

Readings

Acts 2:4
Romans 15:13

Illustration

Have a nice mug which is empty. Get people to admire it, tell them how beautiful it is – but it is useless unless it has something in it – it is no use empty! Only when it has something in it does it fulfil its purpose. People and their minds are the same: we are no use if we are empty.

Borrow a jacket or a fleece, lay it before you and admire it. How good it is for keeping out the cold. Now command it to raise an arm or to sit up straight. When it fails to act, say you know a secret way of getting it to do things. Now get the owner to put it on and raise an arm. The jacket is of no use unless it is occupied.

Nature abhors a vacuum – something will always fill an empty space. Let us all be filled with the Holy Spirit of God.

89 Abundant life

Aim

To show that miracles are mysteries and signs of the kingdom.

Reading

John 10:10

Illustration

Have you ever heard of Dracula? Dracula is supposed to come when you are asleep and drain away your life. When you wake up in the morning you are at least half dead. It is not a true story but sometimes we can wake exhausted; we can feel we have no energy. Human resources do run out. Our batteries need recharging; we need to be refreshed and renewed.

When we feel we have reached the bottom of the barrel we need outside help. There are times when we are unable to help ourselves but Jesus is able to help us. In John 10:10, Jesus says, 'I came that they may have life, and have it abundantly.' You can trace this giving of abundant life, and how Jesus meets various needs and losses of well-being, in John's Gospel:

Need more wine – 2:1-11
Loss of well-being – 4:46-54
Lack strength – 5:2-9
Lack energy (food) – 6:1-14
Lack of security and safety – 6:16-21
Lack of vision and light – 9:1-7
Loss of life – 11:1-44

Jesus meets our drained resources with his generosity and power.

90 Light

Aim

To continue to show signs of the Christ.

Reading

2 Corinthians 4:6

Illustration

Show an array of lights.

An ordinary lamp is useful when the sun goes down for it helps us to see around the house in the dark. A torch is useful for it is the sort of light you can carry around with you and use whenever you need it. Laser light is used in hospitals for surgery and it is also used as a military weapon – laser always has to be used with great care. A security light is good to welcome you home and also to show up any intruders. People who like to sneak about in the dark do not like security lights – especially if linked with a burglar alarm.

The greatest light we have is the sun. Without the sun all life on earth would perish. We need the sun to survive. We also need it to see where we are going. Yet we cannot look directly at the sun and sometimes we cannot even stay in the sunshine without some protection.

In the same way, we cannot behold the full glory of God but Jesus reveals God to us.

91 Natural healing

Aim

To show that Jesus cares for the lonely, rejected and outcast.

Reading

Psalm 103:1-5

Illustration

There was a lady who lived off the west coast of Scotland on one of the islands, the island of Harris, and she had leprosy. She was forced to live alone on the seashore, where she lived off plants and shellfish. She bathed in the liquid off the shellfish and plants. All her flesh became healed and without leprosy. She praised Jesus in these words:

> There is no plant in the ground
> but is full of his virtue.
> There is no form in the strand
> but is full of his blessing.
> Jesu! Jesu! Jesu!
> Jesu! meet it were to praise him.
>
> There is no life in the sea,
> there is no creature in the river,
> there is naught in the firmament,
> but proclaims his goodness.
> Jesu! Jesu! Jesu!
> Jesu! meet it were to praise him.
>
> There is no bird on the wing,
> there is no star in the sky,
> there is nothing beneath the sun,
> but proclaims his goodness.
> Jesu! Jesu! Jesu!
> Jesu! meet it were to praise him.

92 Don't be alarmed

Aim

To know that whatever happens in this world or to us, God is always with us and promises us the victory through Jesus Christ our Lord.

Reading

Matthew 24:6

Illustration

When you go to an airport there are two places with frightening names. There is the 'departure lounge' and the 'terminal'. One is for those who are departing from us and the other is where it all ends! Well, you could look at it that way. Sometimes the departure lounge is a sad place because we are seeing people off whom we might not see again for a long time. But usually it is full of excited people who are going on holiday or going somewhere special. When we come to the terminal, it is not that we are going to stop there. It can be where all traffic is halted but we are going on to a better place. We are not going to stop at the terminal.

I tell you this because Jesus was talking about the end of the world, as we know it. He was pointing out that there are certain signs that point us towards what seems to be the end. But for us it is the beginning of something new. All the troubles are but the birth pangs of the coming of the kingdom. It is easy to quake with fear when we do not know what lies ahead. But we do know who is waiting to meet us. We may fear that we are losing round after round of the battle but in Christ Jesus we are assured the victory will be ours. The terminal will be where we move on to a better kingdom.

93 The glory of the Trinity

Aim

To rejoice in the presence and power of Father, Son and Holy Spirit.

Reading

John 16:12-15

Illustration

To understand the Three in One is quite difficult. St Patrick suggested the shamrock with its three shapes that made one leaf. Clover is much the same. Others have suggested the human being as made up of body, mind and spirit: three parts that you cannot fully separate and yet one being.

You might like to think of the sun. You can see it in the sky and yet it is too bright to look at. In its glory you may like to compare the sun to God the Father. Even when the sun is hidden we know it is still there.

The sun provides the world with light. This light gives life to the world and in the light we can live and move. Let the light remind us of Jesus who is the Light of the World. Even on the dullest of days the sun still provides us with light.

The sun also provides us with warmth. Without the warmth the world would be cold and dead. In the warmth we grow and live. Let the warmth remind us of the Spirit.

Glory, light and warmth – we can talk of them as separate things and yet they are bound together. One would not exist without the other.

94 The kingship of Christ

Aim

To know that Christ is our King and wants us to share in his kingdom.

Reading

Luke 23:33-43

Illustration

In science fiction films there is often a scene when the earth or a space ship is hurtling towards disaster. No human could possible save it. Obviously they try everything they can but they just get more exhausted. Some lose hope altogether. Then a mysterious being enters the story, someone or something from beyond our world. He or she has powers beyond our wildest dreams and can change destruction and disaster into peace, calm and order. The world is restored: the being is thanked and then gone from sight.

This is a salvation story and, although fiction, understands something of our need for salvation. It knows we have no power ourselves to help ourselves. It tells of the love from a being far greater and more powerful than we are and of our salvation. There is such a story in the Gospels and it is not fiction. It is the greatest love story and rescue story of all time and yet we do not always make it our own.

95 Jesus shows God's glory

Aim

To show that in Jesus is revealed the full glory of God, for Jesus is God.

Reading

Luke 9:28-36

Illustration

On the night of 31 August 651, the young man Cuthbert was guarding sheep against robbers and wild animals. He was only 16 years old but possessed a spear and a horse. While he stayed alert and watching, the shepherds slept. The night was clear and full of stars. During the night Cuthbert suddenly saw angels descending to the earth and then ascending, taking with them a holy soul to heaven. Cuthbert sought to awaken the shepherds but they missed seeing what he saw. This made Cuthbert say, 'What wretches we are, given to sleep and sloth, so that we never see the glory of those who watch with Christ unceasingly.' The next day Cuthbert learnt that Aidan had died and he then went and offered himself to become a monk at the monastery of Melrose. True vision nearly always demands obedience and a change of direction.

96 Celebrating women in mission

Aim

To give thanks to God for our mothers and for all who have mothered us. We also give thanks to God for his loving care.

Reading

Exodus 2:1-7

Illustration

I want to tell you of a mother who had no children, yet she had a big family. Her name was Teresa and she was born in Albania. She became a nun and her work took her to one of the largest towns in the world, Calcutta. There are many people in that city and it is overcrowded. Many poor people have nowhere to go and they feed off scraps thrown out by others, often out of rubbish bins. They sleep on the streets, in doorways, under bridges. If they are ill, no one cares for them; there are not enough doctors and nurses. They have no home to go to and no mother to look after them. Teresa tried to help as many as she could and they knew her as Mother Teresa.

One day Mother Teresa saw a woman lying in the road. People were just walking past and ignoring her. Mother Teresa saw the woman was very ill. She tried to get people to help but no one wanted to know. Mother Teresa tried to get her into hospital but the doctor said there was no room for people so poorly. She went to see the health officer and he offered her two very small rooms where she could live with the woman and look after her. She did that until the woman died.

Mother Teresa got lots of women, mothers and nuns together and founded the Missionaries of Charity to care for the ill, the unwanted, for the old, for babies and for unwanted children. Mother Teresa may not have had any children of her own but many people called her Mother and she had one of the largest families on earth.

Mother Teresa often said, 'Let us do something beautiful for God', and this she did time and time again.

97 God's love is his glory

Aim

To explore how God's glory is revealed in the death and resurrection of Jesus.

Reading

John 13:31-35

Illustration

Over 150 years ago no one cared for the lepers on the Hawaiian islands. They were driven out of their homes and even off their island. The lepers were taken to a special island called Molokai. Here they were abandoned on the beach, left to suffer and to die.

One man was anxious to do what he could. He was a Catholic priest, Father Damien. He went to Molokai and was shocked at the state of the lepers. A collection of filthy ramshackle huts housed over 800 lepers. Many were helpless, weak and unable to do anything. Yet in their troubles they had built a small chapel.

Father Damien set to work. He encouraged those who were able to tidy up the mess they lived in, to build better homes and to provide a decent water supply. For 13 years he stayed with the lepers and in the end caught the disease himself. He said he was proud and privileged to be one of them. They wanted him to leave Molokai and receive better attention but he refused. Even in his last illness he gave his blankets to others in their need. He continued to show to the end his love of others, that they were not without hope and that the glory of God was for them as for others.

98 Watching and waiting

Aim

To rejoice in the light of Christ that has come into our world.

Reading

Luke 2:22-40

Illustration

As Simeon waited, his life was one of watchfulness and patience. We see a similar watchfulness in birdwatchers. They place themselves where they believe things will happen. They prepare themselves with binoculars or telescopes. Then they wait, often in silence. This is an attentive waiting, a watchful waiting; they are alert and focused on their hoped-for sighting. There was a man who went in search of a rare owl this way. He waited for three days before it appeared. He saw it only for a few moments but he said he would remember it for the rest of his life. He just had to close his eyes to see it again. He knew what it really looked like. Many of us could learn to be more attentive and watchful towards our God.

99 Glorious humility

Aim

To see that Jesus offers us a new image of power.

Reading

Philippians 2:5-11
Luke 19:28-40

Illustration

In the early twentieth century, the Mahatma Gandhi, dressed in his trademark loin-cloth, presented a curious figure – hardly the stereotypical image of an impressive, powerful leader of a nation! However, he won both the hearts and the respect of the people of India, and many others around the world to this day, who were able to see that he was offering them much more than merely a new leader. This was a radical alternative model of leadership as humble service. More than that, it was based on a way of being which sought to build relationships with others rather than dominate or control them. The devotion he inspired gave him a kind of power of which other leaders could only dream.

Jesus' entry into Jerusalem was also offering the people not merely a new king but a whole new model of kingship – and for everyone who would accept him a new way of being with ourselves, each other and the world.

New life in Christ

100 God's transforming power

Aim

To show God meets our lack of resources with his abundant power and generosity.

Reading

John 2:1-11

Illustration

Charles was a relatively new Christian. He had a good home, a job and a loving family. Not long before it had been all endangered through Charles drinking too often. He said he could not help it. Whenever his resources were low, whenever he felt tired or exhausted, he turned to the bottle. His family were suffering; they did not have enough income to survive on after Charles's drinking. A friend introduced him to Alcoholics Anonymous and also to his local church. The second had an amazing effect. Charles discovered the power of the love and presence of God. Now when resources were low or when he felt exhausted, he turned to rest in God and to be renewed by him. At a Bible study he expressed difficulty with the miracle of changing water into wine. 'But,' he said, 'I know Jesus can change lives. He can turn wine into food on the table and to clothes on our backs.' Jesus has the power to renew and refresh each of us in our lives.

101 Jesus, our light and life

Aim

To show that through Jesus we can be reborn.

Reading

John 3:1-17

Illustration

There are many very clever and capable people (they are often also well-off) who feel they are missing out on something of the fullness of life. Listen to the words of Federico Fellini, the Italian film producer: 'Like so many people I have no religion and I just go sitting in a small boat drifting with the tide. I just go on working, cutting, shooting, editing and looking at life and trying to make others see. Today we stand naked and defenceless, more alone than at any time in history. We are waiting for something – perhaps another miracle, perhaps the Martians, who knows?'

Fellini, like Nicodemus, is in the dark, seeking someone or something that will deliver him from the darkness, from nothingness and death. A deliverer, a Saviour, is needed.

102 The resurrection and the life

Aim

To show Jesus as the resurrection and the life.

Reading

John 11:1-45

Illustration

An American army chaplain tells how the raising of Lazarus affected one marine. There was a Bible study group on board a troopship returning from Japan. After studying this passage, a marine said, 'Everything is pointing at me.' The marine described how he had led a wild life and got into bad trouble. No one knew, except God. He felt guilty. He said his life was ruined and he could not face his family. He felt he was a dead man. 'But after reading this chapter, I have come alive again. I know that this resurrection Jesus was talking about is in the here and now, for he has raised me from death to life.' No doubt this man's troubles were not over, but in meeting Jesus he experienced the resurrection and the life.

103 Jesus leads his flock

Aim

To know Jesus as the Shepherd who leads us to life and life eternal.

Reading

John 10:1-10

Illustration

There is an old Jewish legend about why God chose Moses to be a leader of his people. When Moses was in the wilderness and caring for the sheep of his father-in-law, Jethro, a young lamb strayed away and got lost. Moses searched for it until he came to a deep dark ravine where it had gone down to find water. When Moses got to it he said, 'I did not know you ran away because you were thirsty. Now you must be very tired.' He took the lamb and put it on his shoulders and carried it back to safety. God said to Moses, 'Because you have cared for and brought back one of a flock belonging to man, you shall lead my flock Israel.'

104 Jesus is the way

Aim

To show that Jesus is with us on the journey of life and shows us the way.

Reading

John 14:1-14

Illustration

Often when we are feeling lost it is because we have wandered from him who is the way. More than any book of directions, we need to know God is with us on our journey.

> And I said to the man
> who stood at the gate of the year:
> Give me a light
> that I may tread safely into the unknown.
> And he replied:
> Go out into the darkness
> and put your hand in the Hand of God.
> That shall be to you better than a light
> and safer than a known way.

(From *Desert* by Minnie Louise Haskins, 1908, and quoted by King George VI in his Christmas broadcast, 25 December 1939.)

105 Father, Son and Holy Spirit

Aim

To encourage everyone to be Trinitarian in their faith and their prayers.

Reading

Matthew 28:16-20

Illustration

In the Hebrides, the islands off the west coast of Scotland, it was often difficult for a priest to get to some of the communities to baptise a new-born child. It became the tradition for the midwife to do a form of baptism that was known as the 'birth baptism'; later the child would be baptised in church and this was known as the 'great baptism' or the 'church baptism'. One such midwife said, 'When the image of the God of life is born into the world I put three little drops of water on the child's forehead. I put the first little drop in the name of the Father, and the watching-women say, "Amen." I put the second little drop in the name of the Son, and the watching-women say, "Amen." I put the third little drop in the name of the Spirit, and the watching-women say, "Amen." . . . All the people in the house are raising their voices, with the watching-women giving witness that the child has been committed to the blessed Trinity.'

Here is part of such a baptism prayer:

In the name of God,
in the name of Jesus,
in the name of the Spirit,
the perfect Three of power.

The little drop of the Father
on thy little forehead, beloved one.

The little drop of the Son
on thy little forehead, beloved one.

The little drop of the Spirit
on thy little forehead, beloved one.

To aid thee, to guard thee,
to shield thee, to surround thee.

106 Transformed by his power

Aim

To look at the transforming power and love of Jesus.

Reading

Matthew 9:9-13, 18-26

Illustration

Jim had all the money he needed. It seemed whatever he did turned to gold. He had a great home and a lot of friends. He was able to spend a good deal of time enjoying himself. But Jim had an emptiness that nothing could fill. The more he tried to fill it with action, things or parties, the more it gnawed at him. He told a friend and the friend introduced him to a poem called 'The Hound of Heaven' by Francis Thompson. The line that worried the rich man was 'All things betray thee, who betrayest me'. The friend had the sense to tell him that he need not worry, for the hunger that he felt was none other than the calling of God in his life. 'Listen to God, respond to God and you will soon feel different.' Jim did as advised, he did not change his way of life or his friends, but he turned to God each day, started to worship each Sunday at his local church. He did not change but God changed him and he was now a far richer man than he had ever been.

107 Responding to Jesus' call

Aim

To encourage people to respond to the welcoming call of Jesus and find rest.

Reading

Matthew 11:16-19, 25-30

Illustration

From *The Pilgrim's Progress* by John Bunyan:

> He ran . . . till he came to the place somewhat ascending and on that place stood a cross . . . Just as Christian came up . . . his burden loosed from his shoulders and fell from off his back . . . I saw it no more.
>
> Then Christian glad and lightsome said with a merry heart, 'He has given me rest by his sorrow and life by his death' . . . it was very surprising to him that the cross should ease him of his burden . . . Then Christian gave three leaps for joy, and went on singing,
>
> 'Thus far did I come laden with my sin
> nor could ought ease the grief that was within
> till I came hither: what place is this,
> must be here the beginning of my bliss,
> must here the burden fall from off my back,
> must here the strings which bound it crack.
> Blest Cross! Blest Sepulchre! Blest rather be
> the man who was put to shame for me.'

108 Forgiveness has no limits

Aim

To show there are no limits to God's love and forgiveness.

Reading

Matthew 18:21-35

Illustration

When John Wesley was sailing to America he witnessed the keel-hauling of a member of the crew for an offence on board ship. This was a particularly cruel form of punishment as it meant being tied to a rope, thrown overboard, drawn under the vessel and out the other side. There was always the chance you would drown or perish in some other way. The captain said to John Wesley as they watched, 'You see, Mr Wesley, I never forgive.' It was not for John Wesley to question the captain's power of command but he could and did question that statement. He replied, 'Then, sir, I hope that you never sin!'

109 RSVP

Aim

To show that we are invited to share the joys of the kingdom in the presence of the King, but that it is up to us to accept that invitation.

Reading

Matthew 22:1-14

Illustration

Richard and Judy were invited to the palace to meet the King to enjoy sharing in the beauty of the surroundings and to take part in a banquet. It was a most generous invitation and they wondered what they had done to deserve it. In fact, it was sent out because of the love of the King. They showed lots of people the invitation with pride. They put it where it could be seen in their house. Most days they looked at it and said how wonderful it was. They had advance warning of the date and slowly it came near. One day Judy looked at her calendar and said, 'Oh, I am supposed to get my hair done today – what shall I do?'

Richard replied, 'That's OK. Just go ahead. I fancy doing some gardening.' For all their talk and show, they counted the invitation of little value. By excusing themselves, they excluded themselves.

110 Love's explosion

Aim

To know that we are chosen by God.

Readings

John 1:4-5
1 Thessalonians 4:16-17

Illustration

Once upon a time there was an explosion that radiated out through the world. Countless people were touched, infected: many found it contagious as someone who was already touched passed it on to them. The explosion happened on a hill called Calvary just outside Jerusalem. Here love broke out in great power, defeating darkness. In a flash of blinding love, the Christ released a new way of life for the world. The love of God radiated through the whole earth and all times. The results of that explosion are still being felt today because he who died rose again. He lives and seeks to share his love with us. He comes to us and wants to be our friend. There are always those who will protect themselves against such an event; who will ignore his presence and avoid his radiant love. But he will transform all who come to be touched and give them the power to become the true children of God. They will shine with his presence and his love.

111 Full or empty?

Aim

To see Jesus as the Bread of Life.

Readings

John 6:27
Luke 12:15
Matthew 4:4

Illustration

Throughout our world there are people who seem to have to fill their lives with food, with things or with activity. No matter how much they get, they are still not satisfied. When young people say they are bored, it is usually when they have plenty happening around them but they recognise emptiness within. Bored means having a hole drilled in you. There is something in you that things cannot fill, no matter how you stuff yourself or your days. God made us for himself and nothing else will really fill the space he created within us for himself. In each of us there is a space for the eternal and nothing less than the eternal God can fill it.

112 Sight restored, life renewed

Aim
To show Jesus is the Lord of life.

Reading
Luke 7:11-17

Illustration
Pasha lived in India and his world was slowly getting darker and darker. This was hard enough to bear because his oncoming blindness meant he was losing the ability to enjoy the light of day. Even worse than this, however, was the fact that he would soon be without work due to his loss of sight. Not only Pasha but all his family would suffer. They would join the many poor and marginalised people of India. Then one day it was announced that an 'Eye Camp' was coming to his village. This was run by Sight Savers and was producing wonderful results all over India. Pasha was accepted for what was a relatively simple operation. Afterwards his eyes were bandaged for a few days and, in a sense, he felt worse off. Then came the wonderful moment when the bandages were taken off and he could see. Not only had his sight been saved but also his family had been rescued from poverty. The healing was one for the whole family and they were able to live a fuller life once more.

113 God sends and saves

Aim

To think about how God sends his messengers to us and comes himself in others.

Reading

Hebrews 13:1-8

Illustration

Sadhu Sundar Singh was the first Christian Sadhu. He suffered great persecution in his missionary travels in Tibet. Often the sadhu declared that he was rescued by angels. The following tells of such an occasion.

The sadhu was arrested for entering Tibet and preaching Christianity. The Lama condemned him to death. The sadhu was thrown into a deep dry well. The well was covered and locked. The key was kept around the Lama's waist. The remains of others who had met a similar fate were in the well. The sadhu could not see this because there was no light. For two days and nights he was without food and water. On the third day, when he was exhausted, a wonderful thing happened. He heard the key turn in the lock and the cover was removed. A rope was lowered. It had a loop in the end for the sadhu to put his foot in. He was then gently lifted to the surface. He helped his rescuer to put the cover back on the well. When the sadhu turned to thank him, he was gone. It was only some time later, when the sadhu resumed his preaching, that the Lama discovered what had happened. Yet the key was still fastened at his waist.

I am sure it was a caring human being that rescued the sadhu. Just as I am sure and agree with Sadhu Sundar Singh that it was an angel of God that set him free.

114 It's not about appearances

Aim

To know we are in the hands of God and that he can restore and renew us.

Reading

Jeremiah 18:1-11

Illustration

In the saleroom there was a violin. It looked battered and neglected. One or two people picked it up and pulled the bow across it but the sound did not seem good. The auctioneer wondered why it was in the sale. He thought it should have been scrapped. It looked a sorry sight. Most people never even noticed it. It would probably sell for a few pence.

Just before the sale an elderly gentleman came in. As the seats were filling up he went over to the violin and retuned it. Then he started to play. The music was wonderful. The capabilities of the instrument were amazing. In the master's hand, the poor-looking instrument was transformed.

When the violin was put up for auction the bidding was brisk. People realised it was a precious instrument and that it had great potential. It is amazing how things can be changed in the hands of the master.

115 Christ sets us free

Aim

To show that coming to Jesus gives us a glorious freedom.

Reading

Luke 13:10-17

Illustration

Robert was in prison for repeatedly breaking the law. He was a violent person. Taking drugs fuelled his violence. He was an addict – and that made him a prisoner as much as being in jail. He was not a likeable character and had few friends. Whilst in jail he went regularly to a rehabilitation unit to cure him of his dependence on drugs. Slowly he was freed from the habit. Whilst this was going on he had a regular visit from the prison chaplain. At first Robert rejected him and refused to listen but then he accepted a Bible. One day when he was reading St Luke the tears began to flow. When the chaplain came later Robert showed him the story of the crippled woman and said, 'Jesus has done the same for me. He has set me free.'

116 God's indestructible hope

Aim

To rejoice in the resurrection and newness of life.

Reading

Luke 20:27-38

Illustration

Have you ever been to a butterfly centre? There are a few of them around, mainly in holiday resorts, where you can see all kinds of butterflies at every stage of development. It's fascinating to see how they change from the caterpillar, crawling around the branches, through the chrysalis stage, where they could easily be thought to be dead, later emerging as beautiful butterflies soaring through the air. I often wonder whether caterpillars actually know what they will become, or whether they would find it impossible to believe until it happens.

That's the kind of transformation that resurrection life is about – something so different and amazing that we couldn't possibly imagine it until it happens.

117 Through death to life

Aim

To affirm that whatever happens our God is with us.

Reading

Luke 21:25-36

Illustration

Airports can be sad places for it is where we often say farewell to friends and loved ones who are not coming with us. We see them off and then we go to the 'departure lounge' before going to the 'terminal gate'. Don't you find those words a little threatening, if not downright depressing? You are among the departing and have come to the terminal – it sounds awful! What lifts the spirit is what is beyond. You are not stuck there, for you are off to be with a loved one, to a richer and a fuller life, or escaping from the pressures of work. The terminus is not the end but a place where we get off or set off for somewhere better.

St Luke seeks to tell us that when things come to an end we do not, for our God cares for us and is with us.

118 Love brings new life

Aim

To show that our faith is one of joy and love.

Reading

Philippians 4:4-7

Illustration

There was once a young girl who was always told off at home. Whatever she did, she was criticised (a bit like Cinderella). Nothing could please her parents and they often seemed angry with her. Never did they show their love. The girl felt ugly, she developed asthma and eczema. Later still she went into a psychiatric hospital because she was so depressed and felt useless. It seemed no one could make her better.

One day a hospital orderly noticed that beneath her sad face was a beautiful young woman. When he talked to her she was intelligent and interesting. Soon he formed a relationship with her, bringing her presents and praising the artwork she did. At this she seemed to glow. The orderly got permission to take her out on the odd Saturday. Soon they were deeply in love. Once she knew she was loved she began to smile. Her work was appreciated and soon her eczema and asthma seemed to disappear. There was a new peace and joy in her life. I can tell you she married the orderly and became a good artist. The loving presence of another had transformed her life.

119 From destruction to renewal

Aim

To enter into the joy and wonder of the resurrection and the presence of the risen Lord.

Reading

Luke 24:13-35

Illustration

High up on the moors in the winter season, men go out and set fire to the old heather. By now the heather is all twisted and gnarled; it no longer produces food for the birds and even the moorland sheep are in danger of pulling their teeth out tugging at it. The heather has become useless to the life it usually sustains. So it is burnt, but with a controlled burning. In the flames it may look as if it is totally destroyed but it is not. Under the ground its roots are safe and the men make sure the fire is not too fierce to reach the roots. In the spring the old heather is gone but little shoots appear. The heather is rising from the earth and soon will appear as fresh and as useful as ever. What was destroyed is back with newness of life.

The life of faith

120 Never put off today . . .

Aim

To be awake to Christ's coming to us today.

Reading

Matthew 24:36-44

Illustration

When the devil wanted to ruin the lives of many people he called a meeting of his fallen angels and sought suggestions. 'I will tell them there is no God,' said the first. The devil replied, 'Any sensitive and thinking person knows there is a God and this will not lead them astray.' Asecond said, 'I will tell them there is no hell.'

'What is the use of that?' asked the evil one. 'Everyone will experience a taste of hell and know that it is a reality.'

A third then spoke up and said, 'I will tell them there is no hurry. Put it off until tomorrow – for I know tomorrow never comes.' With this the devil was delighted and this is how most people fail to turn to God.

Pablo Picasso said, 'Never put off today anything that you do not want to leave undone for ever.'

121 Practise what you preach

Aim
To show that actions speak louder than words.

Reading
Matthew 11:2-11

Illustration
When Bede writes about St Aidan he says, 'The highest recommendation of his teaching to all was that he and his followers lived as they taught. He never sought or cared for any worldly possession, and loved to give away to the poor who chanced to meet him whatever he received from kings or wealthy folk. Whether in town or country, he always travelled on foot unless compelled by necessity to ride; and whoever the people he met on his walks, whether high or low, he stopped and spoke to them. If they were heathen, he urged them to be baptised; and if they were Christians, he strengthened their faith and inspired them by word and deed to live a good life and to be generous to others.'

It was the example of a life lived for God that spoke out louder than the words he spoke and backed up what he preached.

122 Perfect freedom

Aim

To show that true freedom comes from loving and serving God.

Reading

Romans 8:18-30

Illustration

Ivan lived under an oppressive regime. If those in power wanted anything, they took it. If they wanted you to do something, you had to do it or your life was at risk. The state police did not knock on doors; they forced their way into people's homes, and if they wanted anything, they took it. Everyone lived in fear and was oppressed. It was during this time that Ivan learnt the Good News of the Gospel. God did not force himself on people. He waited for Mary and Joseph to agree to his plans. In Jesus he did not oppress people but liberated them. Jesus did not burst into lives but said, 'I stand at the door and knock.' Ivan was amazed that so many ignored this loving, saving God. From the moment Ivan heard of such a God he sought to serve in that service which is 'perfect freedom'.

123 Many roads to God

Aim

To take encouragement from the example of the wise men in our own journey of faith.

Reading

Matthew 2:1-12

Illustration

There are many roads to God. God calls each of us and waits for our response. In the wise men we see at least three different roads. Perhaps they travelled alone and on different paths at the outset. Their faith journey brought them together.

Gold is a symbol of all God's gifts. All things come from God and of his own do we offer. God gives us life and this wonderful world. Many come to God through thanksgiving, through gratitude for all that he gives. Gold is also a symbol of power: wealth helps people to achieve and poverty restricts people.

Frankincense is symbol of awe, of mystery and adoration. If we are sensitive to the wonders of the world and the mystery of creation, this can lead us to God. This in turn can lead us to respect all of creation because it is of God. Frankincense is used in worship and many people learn of God through the worship of others.

Myrrh is a symbol of pain and the need for relief from pain and sorrow. For many it is easy to forget God in the good times. But when we lose a loved one or become seriously ill ourselves, it makes us ask questions about our existence. As mortals we all need the salvation and healing that God gives.

124 Bringing others to Jesus

Aim

To show the importance of bringing people to Jesus.

Reading

John 1:29-42

Illustration

It is often proclaimed that the Church is suffering from a crisis in the West. There is a shortage of priests, of ministers. Allied to this is a shortage of money. But more money or more clergy will not cure the crisis. The Church needs a dose of Andrews! It needs people who will abide with Christ and then bring others to Christ. The Church is not short of people and it could grow as it did of old if we would learn to abide with Christ and seek to bring others to him.

The Church grew from twelve disciples who were with Jesus and who wanted others to know him. We must learn to bring others to the One we know and love. Just think how quickly the Church would grow if we were all committed to bringing some-one else to know Jesus.

125 Giving ourselves to God

Aim

To encourage people to respond to the call of God.

Reading

Matthew 4:12-23

Illustration

There are two stories of Socrates and his calling of disciples. Xenophon met Socrates on the road and the teacher barred his path with a stick. Socrates asked Xenophon simple questions about where certain things were made. Then he asked, 'Do you know where men are made good and virtuous?'

'No, I do not,' answered the young man. Socrates then said, 'Follow me and learn.'

On another occasion a man called Aeschines came to Socrates and said, 'I am a poor man, I have nothing else to offer but myself.' Socrates replied, 'Do you not see that you are giving me the most precious thing of all?'

It is in giving ourselves to God that we truly give.

126 The light of Christ

Aim

To let the light of Christ enter our hearts and our lives.

Reading

Luke 2:22-40

Illustration

The night was pitch black as the car drove along a country lane. There were no lights for miles. Suddenly the driver was aware that a rear tyre had a puncture. He would have to stop and mend it. Once out of the car he could see very little. The lights of the car did not give light where he wanted it and he had no torch. This would be a very slow job and he was not sure he could do it in the dark. It was worrying because he was a long way from any houses and it was very late at night. Fortunately, within a few minutes he saw a light coming along the road in front of him. It was a milkman on his early rounds. Though he was busy, the milkman stopped and provided light and what a difference that made. The man no longer worked in darkness but in the light.

127 The light of the world

Aim

To look at what it means to be the light of the world.

Reading

Matthew 5:14-20

Illustration

A man bought a special gift for his wife. It was a musical box that played a tune when you opened it, but it was different because it also glowed in the dark. It was meant to be seen when the days were dark or dull. As it was a present, he kept the box hidden away and all wrapped up. At last he produced it one dark evening and his wife unwrapped it with great excitement. They turned the lights off, but then it could not be seen. It did not glow in the dark, and they were disappointed. Perhaps it was broken. They put the lights back on and discovered a label inside the box that said, 'If you want me to shine all night, keep me in the sun all day.'

There was nothing wrong with the box, and once they left it in the sunlight, it glowed in the dark.

In the same way if we are to be lights in the world, we must spend time each day absorbing the light of Christ.

128 Made in his image

Aim

To show how our lives should reflect the love of God because we are made in his image.

Reading

Matthew 5:43-48

Illustration

One of the Great Masters was painting the Last Supper. The painting was coming along well until he had a violent row with a friend. He went home full of anger and painted on to the canvas his friend as Judas. This would serve to remind him of the row between them; it would keep his anger warm. Now there was little of the painting to finish, only the central character which was the Christ. But the vision would not come. Hand and eye did not work as they should and the canvas was left unfinished. The hatred of the Judas figure was destroying peace of mind and preventing creative work. The anger in the mind left no room for vision. After weeks the canvas was untouched. He met his former friend and now felt ashamed of what he had done. He expressed sorrow to his friend and they were reunited. The artist went home and changed Judas and then painted his friend in the Christ place. The friendship had been restored and so the canvas completed.

129 Temptation

Aim

To show that temptation is the norm if we are truly alive.

Reading

Matthew 4:1-11

Illustration

One of the Desert Fathers prayed that all his passions should be taken away so that he would not be tempted. He then went to one of the Elders and said, 'You see before you a man who is not tempted and is at rest.' The Elder replied, 'Go and pray that some struggle is stirred up in you for the soul only matures through its battles against evil.' The monk did as he was asked and when temptation came he didn't ask to escape it but instead prayed, 'Lord, give me strength to get through the fight.'

Temptation is part of being alive to what is around us. We will be tempted as long as we live.

130 The Prince of Peace

Aim

To know Jesus as the Prince of Peace.

Readings

Matthew 21:1-11
Psalm 118:1, 2, 19-29

Illustration

In a time when in some areas even the wearing of a cross is forbidden, and when the media are often pro-other faiths and anti-Christian, one Anglican bishop made a telling comment. He was asked why the Christians did not threaten with bombings and reprisals as some did. The bishop replied simply, 'We are not allowed to react like that: we follow the Prince of Peace.'

131 Love expressed in action

Aim

To show that loving God demands a response.

Reading

John 14:15-21

Illustration

How often do we fail to realise the cost of love in our homes? How our parents spend much of their lives giving themselves and what they have to us? Many of the household chores that are done for us are done not out of compulsion but out of love. But we should never take this for granted and the only way to respond to such love is to love in return. This, of course, would mean taking our share in the household tasks! Love is expressed in action. We do not do it because we have to – or because it is a rule of the house; we do it out of love for each other. True devotion is taking on some of the routine of caring for our home. Our failure in this work shows a lack of sensitivity and personal response to love.

132 Filled with the Spirit

Aim

To proclaim and enjoy the fact that 'his Spirit is with us'.

Reading

Acts 2:1-21

Illustration

For a long time the flute seemed to lie around the house. It was not played and it gathered dust. Occasionally, someone would get it out and struggle to play a tune. It was decided that is was not a good instrument, perhaps useless and should be got rid of. This was mentioned to a friend of the family when he came to dinner. He asked that he might be able to handle it and play it. Mother had to dust it down before she gave it to him. Somehow it looked special as soon as it was in his hands. Once he started to play, the family were amazed at the beautiful sounds and music. This was a wonderful instrument and responded beautifully in the master's hands. It was just waiting for the touch of the master.

In many ways the disciples were like this until they were filled with the Spirit.

133 Firm foundations

Aim

To encourage the building of a relationship with our God.

Reading

Matthew 7:21-29

Illustration

In the last century the cathedral at Winchester had restoration troubles. Great cracks were appearing in the structure. Experts suggested building buttresses to hold the cathedral up; others suggested great metal tie-bars to be placed across the cathedral to stop its walls falling outwards. One man insisted that they were only dealing with the symptoms of the trouble and the real cause was much deeper: he wanted to look at the foundations. He sunk a shaft into the ground and looked. He discovered the cathedral was built on a peat bog. The builders had laid tree trunks over the watery land and the cathedral was built on these. Due to improved drainage in the city the peat had dried out and shrunk. In many places there was a space between the cathedral and the ground below it. A man was employed for five and a half years to work underground in the removing of peat and putting in its place concrete blocks. Even a cathedral is only as firm as its foundations.

134 Go out in my name

Aim

To show that those whom Jesus calls he also sends out.

Reading

Matthew 9:35–10:8-23

Illustration

Picture yourself coming to your own community and all the lights are out. The only light is coming from the church. You go to see where the light is coming from. It is coming from near the altar, so you approach the light. You see it is coming from a man sitting in a chair. You are about to ask him what he is doing and you see it is the Christ. You kneel before him. He does not move because he is a captive. He is tied to the chair, a prisoner. You ask him, 'Why are you tied, what has fixed you here?'

He replies, 'I am stuck here because my people will not reach out in love. My people do not proclaim the Good News. My people do not help in the healing of the nations. They have fastened me in the building.'

'Lord, how can I set you free?'

'By going out in my name and working with me in all the world.'

You offer yourself to his service, saying, 'Here I am, send me.' At that moment the Christ is freed and the lights begin to come on again.

135 Growing seeds

Aim

To encourage more receptivity in our hearing and receiving of the word.

Reading

Matthew 13:1-9, 18-23

Illustration

In India 150 years ago, in the area of Dornakal, there was a man called Venkaya who could neither read nor write. He heard from a friend about a new religion that was of a God that loved everyone. One day as he watched the Hindu pilgrims bathing in the river he was asked by one of their leaders why he was not bathing. He said he no longer believed enough in the Hindu ways. The leader asked if he was a Christian and Venkaya said, 'No, but I would like to be.' The leader told him of an English Christian preacher who could help him. Venkaya sought out Mr Darling who was a missionary with the Church Missionary Society. At that moment Mr Darling was deeply distressed: he had spoken of Christ for eight years and had not had one convert. Now, amid much opposition, Mr Darling taught and then baptised Venkaya and sixteen other outcasts. The seed was beginning to grow. In his old age and quite blind, Venkaya sat by the roadside to tell others the Gospel story. Through his preaching 500 converts were baptised. His work continues to bear fruit.

136 Weeding out the harmful

Aim

To show that although good and evil are woven into our lives, we must at some stage weed out the harmful.

Reading

Matthew 13:24-30, 36-43

Illustration

They were known as the terrible twins at school. They were disruptive in class and caused no end of bother in the playground. They were encouraging other children to be disruptive too. Staff meetings talked about them, offered ideas to help them, but all were determined to keep them in the class if possible. Teachers used their skill and discernment in dealing with them. It was only in the third year that it became obvious that it could not go on. By then it was also obvious it was not both of them but just one who was the real trouble. They were put in separate year groups. Now one settled down and worked hard. The other continued to be trouble at school and at home. The school finally had to remove the disruptive one from the normal class. They were reluctant to do so but it needed doing. Though they were twins with apparently equal opportunities, one caused trouble all his life; the other became a doctor and a healer.

137 The kingdom of heaven

Aim

To show how we need to search for the kingdom; we need to sow and sift out the good from the bad.

Reading

Matthew 13:(31-33), 44-52

Illustration

Every so often we hear of someone finding a great treasure. These days metal detectors are often used to go over fields and ancient sites to turn up all sorts of wonderful things. Sometimes it is the work of archaeologists who patiently, carefully and slowly remove piles of debris before they get to the treasure they are looking for.

In 1947 a Bedouin shepherd boy was looking for a sheep that had strayed. Spying a cave in the cliff face, he decided to come back with a friend and explore. In the cave they found large earthenware pots with scrolls inside wrapped in linen. They were treasure indeed, for they were the Dead Sea Scrolls and the place was Qumran. In time the scrolls were sold and the boy compensated. All the caves in the vicinity were searched and more scrolls were found. Asect of Jews around the time that Jesus lived had written the scrolls. Many insights into the world that Jesus lived in have come from the deciphering and reading of these scrolls – they are a treasure indeed.

138 Seek first God's will

Aim
To show that we need to resist those, even loved ones, who prevent us from doing the will of God.

Reading
Matthew 16:21-28

Illustration
When the devil cannot get at us directly he will seek to lead us astray by our friends. It is sad how many people are led astray by friends and family. Sometimes our loved ones are only seeking to protect us but in so doing they stop us risking for God.

Columbanus was born in Ireland about 540 AD. He was of noble birth, strong and intelligent and destined to be a ruler of people. Columbanus heard the call of God and decided to dedicate his life to God in a monastery. His poor mother was heartbroken. He could have such a wonderful career and he was hardly ready to leave home. She tried to stop him, at first holding on to him and then lying down across the doorway sobbing. It was very difficult for Columbanus but he had set his sights on serving God. He stepped purposefully over his mother and set out for the monastery. If he had stayed at home, we would never have heard of him, but in time he became one of the greatest missionaries and teachers in Europe.

139 God's generosity

Aim

To show how caring and generous God is.

Reading

Matthew 20:1-16

Illustration

Theo kept strange accounts. He gave equally and generously to all who worked for him. He did not count one worth more than another. All who were willing and able to work were given a whole day's pay whether they had been asked to work all day or only for an hour. It was the same with his relationships: he cared for all equally. Some thought that they clocked up a bigger balance for reward and expected to receive more. But Theo loved all equally. Some grumbled about this but in truth they were trying to buy his love and affection when it was freely given to all. There are always people who grumble.

The only people Theo could not help were those who chose to turn away from him. Even these he gladly would give to if they allowed him to. Theo kept strange accounts.

140 Words and deeds

Aim

To look at making choices and practising what we profess.

Reading

Matthew 21:23-32

Illustration

In a community there was a group of people who were always ready to say, 'Yes, sir. Three bags full, sir.' They appeared to be willing to take on anything that was asked and always talked with respect. They appeared only too willing, ready and able. But when it came to the crunch they were too busy, too tired, couldn't be bothered, or had just forgotten what they had promised. When they were needed they did not turn up.

There was another group who always seemed reluctant. They did not particularly want to get involved. They had other things to do. Yet when they were aware of the need they had a change of heart and waded in. They would not profess to be part of any system, but out of love and care they got on board and did what was needed.

It was hard to depend on either group but in the end the second group was more likely to get things done.

141 Care for God's world

Aim

To appreciate all that God has given us and act responsibly.

Reading

Matthew 21:33-46

Illustration

The group was given a new hall through the generosity of others and through national grants. But from the start they did not appreciate it. The walls were daubed with graffiti, the floor was covered with litter; inside the building they ran riot. Though people tried to care for them, they rejected any offers of oversight or help. In time the hall looked derelict and no one dared to go and look after it. Windows were broken and toilets were vandalised.

Sadly after all the efforts of some the hall was shut down. Those who were given it were causing too much trouble. It became a liability. The idea had been a good one but the group did not appreciate this. Finally it was dismantled and the land given to others.

142 Give God his due

Aim

To show that we must give God his due.

Reading

Matthew 22:15-22

Illustration

Some of the greatest witnesses to giving God his due were the early Christian martyrs. Catherine, who gives her name to the 'Catherine Wheel' firework, was born of a noble family and lived in the fourth century. The emperor was attracted to her and wanted to marry her. Catherine refused because she was already a 'bride of Christ'. She is said to have disputed with 50 philosophers whose job it was to convince her of her error and she defeated them. Because she refused to do as commanded by the emperor she was tortured by being fastened to a large wheel and driven around the arena – but the wheel broke. Finally she was beheaded.

143 Love your neighbour

Aim

To encourage us to love God with our whole being.

Reading

Matthew 22:34-46

Illustration

'Christmas wouldn't be Christmas without any presents,' Jo had grumbled as she waited with her three sisters until their mother returned from church . . .

'Merry Christmas, Marmee! Many of them!'

'Merry Christmas, little daughters! But I want to say one word before we sit down. Not far away from here lies a poor woman with a little newborn baby. Six children are huddled into one bed to keep from freezing, for they have no fire. There is nothing to eat over there, and the oldest boy came to tell me they are suffering from hunger and cold. My girls, will you give them your breakfast as a Christmas present?'

They were all unusually hungry having waited nearly an hour, and for a minute no one spoke – only a minute, for Jo exclaimed impetuously, 'I am so glad you came before we began!'

'May I go and help to carry the things to the poor children?' asked Beth eagerly.

'I shall take the cream and the muffins,' added Amy, heroically giving up the articles she most liked.

Meg was already covering the buckwheats, and piling the bread into one big plate.

'I thought you would do it,' said Mrs March, smiling as if satisfied. 'You shall have bread and milk for breakfast and make up for it at dinner time.'

They were soon ready, and the procession set out.

Fortunately it was early and they went through the back streets, so few people saw them, and no one laughed at the queer party.

A poor bare miserable room it was with broken windows, no fire, ragged bedclothes, a sick mother, wailing baby and a group of pale, hungry children huddled under one old quilt to keep warm.

How the big eyes stared and the blue lips smiled as the girls went in!

'Ach mein Gott. It is good angels come to us!' said the poor woman crying for joy.

Little Women, Louisa May Alcott (1868)

144 Due care and attention

Aim

To show how we need to keep ourselves aware that Jesus comes to us.

Reading

Matthew 25:1-13

Illustration

John could have learnt much more at school but he was always fooling around or thinking about what he was going to do after school. He never listened. He was there in body but not in mind or spirit.

Jean knew it was no use talking to her father while he was watching a football match on the television. He was in the same room but he was not really where she was and he would not hear.

There is a danger that we are never really aware of our Lord's coming and we miss the wonderful relationship that is offered to us: we miss the moment even though it is offered to us more than once. Too often Jesus finds we are 'not there' when he comes. He seeks us out but we do not give him any attention. Think of Jesus saying:

> I called your name but you were out or preoccupied.
>
> I came to you in the night but you did not notice.
>
> I knocked on your door and your heart but they remained closed.
>
> I asked for your help but you were too busy.
>
> I wanted to know you, to give my love to you, but you were otherwise engaged.

145 Use it or lose it

Aim

To encourage the awareness that we all have talents to share and develop, and that we must use them.

Reading

Matthew 25:14-30

Illustration

Millie was now quite old but she always had a strange attitude to gifts. If she was given a present, she would thank the person profusely and say how kind it was of them to give her a gift. She said she would treasure it. Then without unwrapping it she put it away in a drawer for another day. When a niece came to help her to move she discovered many unused gifts, still wrapped. There were biscuits and cakes that had moulded away; there were jars of things that had long passed their sell-by date; there were clothes that now would no longer fit Millie. Drawer after drawer of gifts were put out in the bin. Because she did not use them she lost them; she never had the benefit of them.

In the same way we will lose our local small shops unless we use them. We will lose bus services unless we use them. We will lose our God-given gifts and talents unless we use them. The thing we need understand is 'Use it or lose it'.

146 As you did to the least of these

Aim

To make people aware that Christ comes to us in our encounter with others and in the needs of the poor.

Reading

Matthew 25:31-46

Illustration

Christopher wanted to serve the King. He wanted to go to the palace and give himself to serve the King. But he was held up. First he had to look after ageing parents. When he set off he had a gift for the King but he met a poor family who had been robbed of their belongings and he gave the gift to them. Later on he met a family whose cart had stuck deep in the mud. He stayed to help them and got sprayed with mud. Now he had no gift and his fine clothes were filthy. He felt he could not journey on but something encouraged him – words he had heard long ago. When he finally reached the palace, he received a royal welcome. He was about to apologise for the state he was in but the King said, 'You have been a great help to me over the years, in the way you cared for your parents, in the way you gave to the poor and when you helped those in need. I was there and it was me you gave your help and love to. Welcome to the fullness of the kingdom which you have served for a long time.'

147 Help is on the way

Aim

To encourage people to see that Jesus comes in acts of kindness and righteousness.

Reading

John 1:9-13

Illustration

Once upon a time there was a man who went out to sea in a little boat. It was a lovely day and he was enjoying himself. Then the mist suddenly came down. Now he did not know which direction he was going in. He rowed around until he was very tired, then he let himself drift. He did not know that he was drifting towards the rocks. Suddenly he heard a crunch and a scraping. His boat was torn on the rocks and it began to sink. Fortunately he managed to escape on to the rocks. He was now very cold and hungry and he prayed to God to come and rescue him.

Soon a motorboat came by and invited him aboard – but he refused, saying, 'I have help coming.' A little later a fishing boat saw him and tried to persuade him to come off the rock but again he said, 'There is no need to worry I have help on the way.'

That night the man died alone in the cold. He went to heaven and complained to God that he had not come to help. God said, 'I came in a motorboat and you refused my help. I came again in a fishing boat and you still refused my help. You are here today because you did not recognise my help when it came – yet still you are loved.'

148 The Promised Land

Aim

To show that Jesus is the Son of God and fulfils the longings of the law and the prophets.

Reading

Deuteronomy 8:7-10; 34:1-8

Illustration

The day before the civil rights campaigner Martin Luther King was killed by a sniper's bullet he said words of encouragement to a large crowd:

> We've got difficult days ahead. But it does not matter to me now. Because I have been to the mountain top, I won't mind. Like anyone else I would like to live a long life . . . but I am not concerned about that now. I just want to do God's will. And he's allowed me to go up the mountain. And I have looked over and seen the Promised Land. So I am happy tonight, I am not fearing any man. Mine eyes have seen the glory of the coming of the Lord.

Like Martin Luther King, if we are to survive dark days, we need to have a vision of the glory of our God.

149 Obeying God's call

Aim

To encourage people to be faithful to their Lord.

Reading

Luke 14:26-27

Illustration

When Columbanus wanted to go and serve God as a monk his mother was not pleased. She loved him dearly and was afraid that he was wasting his life. He had lots of talent and ability. He could be someone very important in Ireland. She talked to him and tried to dissuade him, but he knew God was calling him to leave home and serve him in a monastery. His mother tried all sorts of ways to stop him. Though she loved him dearly, she was acting for Satan. Columbanus got ready to go. His mother went to the door of the house and lay down in the doorway to stop him. Columbanus was very sorry to see his mother do this, but he carefully stepped over her and went to serve God wherever God called him. In time, Columbanus did wonderful work for God in France and Italy. For a moment it would have been easy to give in and stay at home.

150 Good rules

Aim

To show we are accountable for our actions.

Readings

Matthew 5:17-19
John 2:13-22

Illustration

There was a farmer who planned to go to France for his holidays. As he would be driving on the Continent he decided to get some practice in. He started to drive on the right-hand side of the road and to go around roundabouts anticlockwise. To say the least, he caused all sorts of trouble and had one or two close accidents. He was finally stopped by the police and charged with dangerous driving. He had broken dozens of rules in the Highway Code, and that mattered because it is written for the well-being and safety of us all. We need rules to protect us and to help us to get the best out of life. Rules are not to restrict us as much as to give us the greatest freedom within certain parameters.

What if there were no rules in a game of football? You could have as many people as you like on your team. You could pick up the ball and run or even take it home! You could make the goal-posts narrower than the football so that no one could score. But you would not have a game; you would have chaos. We need rules and standards to enjoy living together in community.

Jesus was angry with the moneychangers because they were being unjust. They were using their privileged position to make unfair demands. They were robbing people in the name of God. Jesus could not turn a blind eye. He had to act. He had to show that what was being done was not right and needed to be changed. Perhaps on a larger scene Jesus was already hinting that the time for animal sacrifices had come to an end and that a great sacrifice was about to be made in his own crucifixion.

151 Evangelism

Aim

To show we are one with Christ and that we are called to bear fruit.

Readings

Acts 8:4+, 26-40
Isaiah 53

Illustration

We hear little of the disciples after the resurrection but we know they all bore the fruit of being with Jesus. After the death of Stephen, the disciples scattered because of persecution. We know Philip went to Samaria and told the story of Jesus. He preached of the love of God. Through the disciples the Church was growing rapidly and beyond the boundaries of Jerusalem (see Acts 8:4+). Peter and John also went to the Samaritans.

A road from Jerusalem went by Bethlehem and, just south of Gaza, joined the main road to Egypt and beyond. St Luke points out that this is the Old or Desert Gaza, not the more modern one. Along this road travelled the Chancellor of the Exchequer of the queen of Ethiopia. He had been to Jerusalem to worship. He is at least a seeker of God. He was in his chariot reading Isaiah 53. Philip simply asked if he understood what he was reading. The Ethiopian said how could he without a guide? Philip was invited into the chariot and they looked at the words: 'He was led like a lamb to the slaughter.' Philip talked of Jesus of the crucifixion and resurrection. The Ethiopian was moved and wanted to be baptised in the nearby water. After being baptised the Ethiopian went on his way rejoicing. Again we see Philip bearing fruit as he does the work of Jesus. Tradition has it that the Ethiopian went home and started to evangelise Ethiopia. And through the witness of many the Church grew in the faith and in number.

152 Oliver's request

Aim

To show the importance of knowing Jesus personally.

Reading

Hebrews 7:19b, 25

Illustration

In the film *Oliver!*, Oliver Twist is in the poorhouse with many other young people. They want someone to complain that they are hungry and want more food. In this case no one wants to do it for they know they are likely to be punished. They decided to pick straws and whoever draws the shortest straw has to do it. If you draw the shortest straw, it means you are chosen. Oliver draws the shortest straw. The others have elected him. So though he is frightened, he goes to the front and asks for more. 'Please Sir, I would like some more.' In the poorhouse this is unthinkable and, as the young people expected, Oliver is punished for asking.

153 The greatness of God

Aim

To encourage a greater awareness of the Trinity.

Readings

Psalm 145:3

Romans 11:33-36

Illustration

A child went down to the beach and dug a hole in the sand. She then went down to the sea and brought some water to fill the hole. In a moment the water disappeared. She went back for more water, and then more. But the same thing happened each time. The little girl became exhausted and began to cry. Meanwhile the tide had been coming in. Her father showed her how to make a channel for the sea, so that it would flow naturally into the hole and fill it. We are like the little girl: we try to fill our minds with ideas about God and often exhaust ourselves. We talk too much. We need learn to wait upon God, knowing he will come to us. Trying to understand the Trinity is like trying to pour the whole sea into a small hole. Yet we can rest in the Trinity and enjoy the love of Father, Son and Holy Spirit.

154 Risk

Aim

To show how Jesus risked safety and security for us.

Reading

Mark 3:1-6

Illustration

Jesus risked his own safety and security for us. As Christians, we are often called to share in this risky adventure. The call is often like the call to the man with the withered hand: 'Come forward . . . stretch out' (Mark 3:3, 5).

Very often the Church hides behind set services and conventions. The words and the patterns are fixed so that no one is disturbed. Jesus calls, 'Come forward.' Stand where everyone can see you. Where every fault-finding eye can fall upon you. Where those who reject Jesus can vent themselves upon you. 'Safety first' is not our policy: the Church is not meant to be hidden – 'Come forward' for Jesus. Then 'stretch out', even if you feel your talent has withered. Attempt the impossible for God, trusting in his power. Take risks for God and let him work through you. The call of Jesus to the man with the withered hand is a call to the Church to let him work through us. Come forward . . . stretch out.

155 Sowing seed

Aim

To show that the kingdom of God is waiting to grow in us.

Reading

Matthew 13:3

Illustration

Jonathan Chapman used to travel around farms in America with his Bible. In the evenings he would read to the family; not many of them could read themselves. They looked forward to his visits and they called him 'Johnny Appleseed'.

This is how he got his nickname. On some farms he noticed the men busy making cider. The apples were pressed and when the juice was extracted the pips were thrown away. 'What a waste,' thought Johnny: those little pips could grow into fine trees. So Johnny asked if he could have some seed. The man replied he could have as much seed as he wanted. Johnny filled his saddlebag with seeds. When he visited a farm, in the evening he read from the Bible, then before he left he would make some holes in the soil and plant some apple seeds. He then made a little fence around them to protect them and to give them the chance to grow. For over 40 years Johnny did this work, sowing the word of God in the hearts of people and sowing apple seeds in the ground. Everywhere he went he left something behind to give pleasure and nourishment to the farming people. He understood well that seeds could not grow unless they were planted.

156 Freedom

Aim

To show Jesus has work for us but will not force himself or his work upon us.

Reading

Revelation 3:20

Illustration

In the totalitarian state you are not allowed free choice. You must do as you are told. If you do not open your door to the officials, it will be broken down. You cannot hide because they will seek you out and make you do what they want.

Jesus is different. He has the power but he will not force himself upon you. The choice is yours: he respects your free will. You can edge him out of your life and home if you so choose. You can be too busy to bother to keep in contact with him if you so desire. He will not force you.

Have a large print of Holman Hunt's picture 'The Light of the World'. If you look at it you will see the door has not been opened for a long time. Jesus stands there knocking and waiting to bring his light upon those who live within. There is no means of opening the door from the outside. If he is to enter, you have to let him in. It is good to think of these words of Jesus every day: 'Behold, I stand at the door and knock' (Revelation 3:20).

157 Is it worth the effort?

Aim

To show the care and concern of Jesus.

Reading

Matthew 10:42

Illustration

There is a story about a boy walking along a beach. All along the shore there were thousands of starfish washed up. You could hardly walk on the sand for them. The boy was putting a few in his bucket and taking them back to the sea. A man came along and said, 'There are thousands of starfish stranded. Why do you bother? You will hardly make an impression. You will only be able to put a few back into the sea.' The boy replied. 'It will matter for these few and it will matter to me.'

Though our effort may be small, it is counted as worthwhile, and who knows what God will do with it?

158 Dying of analysis

Aim

To show the calling of God and the stalling of our hearts.

Readings

Psalm 63:1
Acts 17:28
John 6:35, 41-51

Illustration

There was a brilliant scientist who was keen on analysis. He wanted to get to the basic elements of everything. A meal was set before him and he was hungry. But he wanted to check where this food came from and what was in it. He went into his laboratory and started on a loaf of bread. He did not eat any. He checked what its constituents were. He discovered wholemeal flour, water, yeast, vegetable fat, preservatives, emulsifiers and vinegar. He checked out the preservatives and found calcium propionate and potassium sorbate. By now he was starving but research must go on. The emulsifiers kept him busy for ages. He found mono- and diacetyl tartaric acid, esters of mono- and diglycerides, fatty acids. He was kept very busy but he grew weaker and weaker. He still had to analyse the wholemeal and check out the grains. Sadly he died of starvation whilst looking at the loaf. There was food all around him but he died of analysis.

159 A Godless church

Aim

To encourage our church to be open and welcoming.

Reading

James 2:1-5

Illustration

There was once a very famous church. Every Sunday it was fashionable to go there and be seen. People came in their finery. Some of the most important people of the land attended it. The music and the choir were superb, the ordering of the service was of a very high standard; everything done was to the highest degree of excellence and in the best possible taste. For a good few Sundays a poorly dressed and shabby-looking person turned up at the door but was turned away for one reason or another. After a few weeks of trying to get in, the woman sat on the lowest step and prayed to God, 'Lord, why can I not get entrance into this church?' The Lord replied, 'My daughter, how do I know? I have been trying to get into this church for years.'

160 Obeying the vision

Aim

To encourage a personal relationship with Christ the living Lord.

Readings

Acts 26:19
Mark 3:31-35
Luke 2:48-50

Illustration

In his poem 'Gareth and Lynette', Tennyson tells of the struggle Gareth has to leave home. He wants to become one of the knights of Arthur but his mother does not want him to leave home. She has already lost two of her sons to Arthur's court. 'Hast thou no pity on my loneliness?' she asks. 'Stay, my best son, ye are yet more a boy than a man,' she pleads. The mother produces excellent reasons for Gareth to stay at home and ignore his vision. Here, the tempter is using someone who loves him dearly to stop Gareth serving his vision. Gareth replies:

> O Mother,
> How can you keep me tethered to you – Shame.
> A grown man I am, a man's work I must do.
> Follow the deer? Follow Christ the King,
> Live pure, speak true, right wrong, follow the King –
> Else, wherefore born.

Gareth was not tempted through his mother but followed the vision as he saw it.

161 The fourth wise man

Aim

To show that Jesus calls us to serve each other rather than to lord it over people.

Reading

Matthew 25:34-40

Illustration

There is a story about a fourth wise man who wanted to come and see the Christ. He started off well. He dressed in his best clothes, rode a fine horse and brought a present of precious stones. On his journey he met a group of poor people who were hungry, so he gave away half of his jewels for them to trade for food. Then he met a family who were taken into slavery because of a debt. He used the rest of his precious jewels to buy their freedom. Further on he found a merchant in deep distress. His horse had died on him and he would not get his goods to be sold on time. The generous wise man gave him his horse and all its trappings. Now he had to walk on foot and the going was slow.

He was old and very weary. He wondered if he would ever see the Christ. The way was very muddy and he met a young family trying to get their cart out of the mud. The wise man helped them but ended up very dirty. He now wondered if he should give up and go home. In a dream he was told, 'The Christ you seek is now only a little distance away. He will welcome you because he knows you. You have met him many times on your journey in the poor and the needy. You soiled your clothes in caring for him. Tomorrow you will meet him and he will welcome you.' And so it was.

162 Self-giving

Aim

To show that God wants all of us and not just gifts and prayers.

Reading

1 Corinthians 13:3

Illustration

Imagine a table. I want you to put on it all the things you want to give to God: your time, talents, money; your home, your friends, your loved ones; your job, your plans, your future.

You are going to need a great big table. We raise up the things we want to give to God and say, 'All things come from you, O God, and of your own do we give you.'

But wait, one thing that God wants is still missing. Who knows what it is?

GOD WANTS YOU.

More than any gift, more than gold or silver, God wants you.

God wants you to give yourself to him.

God wants you to give your love.

God wants you more than anything.

St Paul said, 'If I give away all my possessions . . . but do not have love, I gain nothing' (1 Corinthians 13:3).

163 Serving the poor

Aim

To compare the ambition of James and John and the servant role of Jesus.

Reading

Proverbs 14:31; 19:17

Illustration

When Toyohiko Kagawa, who lived in Japan, met Christianity he was captured by its call to serve. He prayed, 'O God, make me like Christ.' To become like Christ he went to live in the slums of Kobe to care for others. He chose to live in a shed that was about two metres square. On the very first night he was asked to share his room and bed with a man with a contagious itch, the first test of his aim to serve. He welcomed the poor man. Then a beggar asked for his shirt and he gave it. The next day the beggar came back for Kagawa's coat and trousers. Kagawa gave them and was left wearing a ragged kimono. At first the slum dwellers laughed at him but they soon came to admire him. Kagawa wrote:

> God dwells in the lowliest of men. He sits on the dust heap among the prison convicts. He stands with the juvenile delinquents. He is there with the beggars. He is among the sick; he stands with the unemployed. Therefore let him who would meet God visit the prison cell before going to the temple. Before he goes to church let him visit the hospital. Before he reads the Bible let him visit the beggar.

164 Lantern Saints

Aim

To rejoice in God's saints.

Reading

Matthew 5:16

Illustration

The Lantern Saints were a group of early Methodists who lived on the North Yorkshire Moors. They had a meeting place on one of the highest points of the moor at Trough House at the head of Fryup Dale. And people came from outlying farms and hamlets, from the dales of Westerdale, Danby Dale, Farndale, Glaisdale, Rosedale and Great and Little Fryup. It made Trough House look like the centre of a web that spread out into each moorland valley. Often in the winter they struggled up to the moorland height and met in a shuttered room. As each family entered they would light their lantern (a good symbol of receiving the light of the Gospel and the Light of Christ). Once the service was over they would set off in every direction. You could see the light they had received and carried with them travelling to each dale, to farms and homes. From that light they would see in the dark and light other lights. This light was a symbol of how they sought to live by the Light of Christ. These ordinary folk were rightly known locally as the 'Lantern Saints'.

165 Prayer-based faith

Aim

To encourage people in their use of intercessory prayer.

Reading

Luke 7:1-10

Illustration

Martin's father was a tribune in the Roman army. This meant he was a man of authority and had charge over six centurions and 600 men. When Martin was 10 years old he went to church and declared he wanted to learn the Christian faith. His pagan parents were not well pleased. The church was attractive to this young mind as the church often is to young folk. By the time he was 15 Martin was often engaged in church work. Not long after this the recruitment age for the Roman army was lowered to 16. Martin's father saw this as an opportunity and got the recruitment officer to call. He came unannounced and with manacles to take Martin off to the army. Now he would have to spend the next 25 years as a soldier. This was not a barren time for Martin. Here he would learn of discipline, obedience and orderliness. He would learn of the need to travel lightly without too many possessions, and because they were often on the move celibacy was the ideal. As the son of an officer he was soon given a commission and was allowed a servant. He shocked others by taking it in turns with his servant to clean their boots. He gave his money to the poor and cared for the needy. It was at the city gates of Amiens that Martin cut his cloak in half and gave half to a beggar.

That same night in a dream he heard Christ say to the angels in heaven, 'Look what Martin, who is still a catechumen, has given to me this day,' and showed them the cloak. Only later would Martin be baptised. Here was a Roman soldier who showed a living faith and a vital relationship with Jesus.

166 Grace is not cheap

Aim

To show that Jesus calls us to follow him and asks for our commitment.

Reading

Luke 9:51-62

Illustration

Dietrich Bonhoeffer was a German Lutheran priest who was executed by the Nazis for his resistance to their evils. He says this concerning the cost of discipleship:

> Cheap grace is the deadly enemy of the Church . . . cheap grace is the preaching of forgiveness without requiring repentance, baptism without church discipline, communion without confession, absolution without contrition. Cheap grace is grace without discipleship, grace without the cross, grace without Jesus Christ, living and incarnate.

167 The mission of the seventy

Aim

To explore the mission of the seventy.

Reading

Luke 10:1-11, 16-20

Illustration

Picture coming home on a dark night. All the lights are out in the whole area. There must have been a power cut. Everyone is in the dark. The only glimmer of light comes from the church. You are a bit nervous and you go in. There is someone sitting in the sanctuary and he is surrounded by light. You sneak forward and see that he has nail marks in his hands and feet. You know it is the Christ but his feet are fastened by chains and his hands are tied. The Christ is unable to move. You come close and ask, 'Lord, your feet are fastened and your hands tied – why?' The Christ replies, 'My feet are fastened and my hands tied because my people do not pray regularly. They do not reach out to others in love. They do not share in my saving works. I have entrusted my work to them and they have not accepted the light I have offered them. Things will only change when you share with me: when you see Christ in others and be Christ to others.' Suddenly you are aware of this truth, and lights start coming on all over the place.

168 Dedication and practice

Aim

To show we need to be active in our faith and that we need to practise.

Reading

Hebrews 11:29–12:2

Illustration

There were two brothers. Both were runners. One was very good and won most races when he was small. He always used to beat his brother. Because he could run well, he decided he did not need to train. It was more fun playing computer games and going out with his friends. He thought practising was a waste of time. The other brother knew that he had to improve his style. He practised often. He practised sprinting and long-distance running. He did exercises to increase his breathing powers and his physical ability. He was seen on the track most nights. His brother said he was wasting his time. By the time they were in their teens, the brother who had been the best now lagged far behind. He was paying the price for not practising and keeping his eyes on what he could do. His brother was now winning competitions and all sorts of prizes. If asked how he became a better runner, he said, 'By a lot of practice and by being willing to dedicate myself to the job.'

169 The communion of saints

Aim

To rejoice in the communion of saints.

Reading

Luke 6:20-31

Illustration

A man presented himself to the minister leading the service once it was over. 'I would like to become a Christian.' The minister enquired what had brought him to this decision. Was it a sermon, a book or some event in his life? The man was a little embarrassed at this point and said how he read little and hardly ever attended church. 'It's my boss at work – he is a real tough chap and we are a hard bunch of men – it's the way he deals with us. I wanted to know what made him so sensitive and caring, what made him strive to be honest and fair to all. He told me it was because he was a Christian. If that is what a Christian is like, that is what I want to be.'

The best advertisement for God and for our faith is the way we live and witness to what we believe.

170 Faith on a cheerless day

Aim

To show that, though troubles will come, our God is with us.

Reading

Luke 21:5-19

Illustration

Life was often bleak for the people who lived in the Hebrides. Sometimes the future did not seem to hold any promise and when the mists came down it did not help. Here is an affirmation prayer that faces the reality of the cheerless day but also a much deeper reality of the love of God and our future in him.

> Though the dawn breaks cheerless on this isle today,
> my spirit walks in a path of light.
> For I know my greatness.
> Thou hast built me a throne within thy heart.
> I dwell safely within the circle of thy care.
> I cannot for a moment fall out of thine everlasting arms.
> I am on my way to thy glory.
>
> *Alistair Maclean, Hebridean Altars*

171 Temptation is everywhere

Aim

To encourage people to face temptation with faith.

Reading

Luke 4:1-13

Illustration

Anyone who is still alive is tempted, so do not say you are not tempted. If you are not tempted, you have never lived or you have let something in you die. There is always a tug of war between good and evil, between achieving and failing to do so. There is no place or person free from this battle. In the book *Rogue Herries*, Hugh Walpole tells of how Herries had come to the wild and lonely Lakeland where he met a travelling preacher called Robert Finch. Herries asked:

> 'How shall I like this place? It is cut off from the world.'
>
> There was a sudden odd note of scorn in the little man's voice as he answered, 'It is the world, sir. Here within these hills, in this space of ground is all the world. I thought that while I was with my Lord Petersham that the world was there, but in every village I have passed since then I have found the complete world – all anger and vanity and covetousness and lust, yes, and all charity, goodness and sweetness of soul. But most of all, here in this valley I have found the whole world. Lives are lived completely . . .The mountains close us in. You will find everything here, sir. God and the devil both walk in these fields.'
>
> *Rogue Herries*, Part 1, by Hugh Walpole

172 Trusting God's promise

Aim

To show how God can be trusted to keep his promises.

Reading

Genesis 15:1-12, 17, 18

Illustration

In a dream a man was told where there was treasure hidden in a nearby castle under a blue stone. The dream was quite clear and he could remember every bit of it. Yet he did not bother even to see if the stone was there in the castle. He told his dream to a friend. His friend went immediately and found a great treasure under the blue stone. He became very rich and although he was generous toward his friend, his friend realised that because he had not bothered when an opportunity was offered him he had missed out in a big way.

How often do we miss out on the fullness of life because we do not take up the promises of our God?

173 A life of purpose

Aim

To show how our lives have purpose and are meant to be useful.

Reading

Luke 13:1-9

Illustration

Abraham Lincoln triumphed over many adversities to become the President of the United States. Here are some of his words and they are about all of life and not just gardens:

> Die when I may, I want it said of me that I plucked a weed and planted a flower wherever I thought a flower would grow.

Think of the purpose of our existence as expressed by The Shorter Catechism of 1647:

> What is the chief end of man?
> To enjoy God and to glorify him for ever.

174 Living to God's glory

Aim

To show that if we are faithful in small things, then we will be trusted to do greater things.

Reading

Luke 5:1-11

Illustration

Denzil was always talking of giving glory to God. The house he lived in was a tip. Every room was untidy if not unclean. Denzil continued to talk of praising God but gave little respect to the people around him. He seemed unaware of his surroundings or of others, only full of himself. One night he heard God in his dreams saying, 'If you want to serve me, start where you live. Give glory to me by tidying up your part of the world. You will hear me better if you learn to listen to others.' Denzil awoke, aware of how ugly his room looked. That day he started to clean up and get rid of rubbish. Soon he redecorated the room and added fresh curtains. He scrubbed himself and got new clothes. He seemed to be a different person: he actually glowed. If someone needed a person to listen or to care, Denzil was the one. By being attentive to small things, God had called him to do greater things for him.

175 Freedom in giving and receiving

Aim

To show that Jesus wants us to have the glorious freedom of the children of God.

Reading

Luke 6:27-38

Illustration

In the Holy Land there are two seas, the Sea of Galilee and the Dead Sea. The same river, the Jordan, feeds both of these seas. The Sea of Galilee teems with life: there are fish in its waters, trees grow near its shoreline, birds visit it and their singing can be heard. The Dead Sea lives up to its name: it does not sustain life, it is too salty to allow plants to thrive and the birds do not like its saltiness. One sea has life and the other is dead, yet the same river feeds both. What is the difference? The answer is quite simple: the river Jordan flows into one end of the Sea of Galilee and out of the other. As the Sea of Galilee receives, so it gives out. The Dead Sea does not have an outlet. All the water that flows into the Dead Sea is kept; it does not give out. The sun evaporates the water and the salts are left behind. Because the Dead Sea does not have an outlet, it dies. By keeping all that it receives, it chokes itself of life. Sadly there are people just like that.

176 Hearing the Shepherd's voice

Aim

To explore our relationship with Jesus through the image of the shepherd.

Reading

John 10:22-30

Illustration

Two flocks of sheep had become intermingled. Night was coming down and it would be very difficult to separate them before it was dark. If men or dogs were sent in, it would cause a lot of fear among the sheep and greater confusion. The shepherd who came to care for his flock said, 'Leave them alone. Wait until it is almost the end of day, then I will call mine. They know me, they will hear my voice and follow me.' As evening came, the shepherd started to call. The reaction among the sheep was interesting, for some heard the voice and wanted to run away because they did not know it. The sheep that belonged to the shepherd recognised his voice. They heard a call that meant safety, shelter and sustenance. They knew of the love of the shepherd and came running to where he was.

177 Deepening our relationship with God

Aim

To seek to deepen our relationship with God.

Reading

Luke 17:5-10

Illustration

George Matheson looked forward to a good life. He was studying for the ministry. He was preparing to marry the one he loved. Then he began to go blind. His world began to go into darkness. He lost many of his friends, and his loved one decided she could not cope with a blind man and left him. His world was shaken but not his relationship with God. George Matheson wrote the hymn 'O Love that will not let me go'. The second verse is 'O Light that follow'st all my way' and the third 'O joy that seekest me through pain'. George had faith in a great God. The final verse 'O Cross that liftest up my head' affirms not only his steadfast relationship but God's relationship with him. Now *that* is faith.

178 God's gift of peace

Aim

To show that Christ is the Prince of Peace.

Reading

Luke 8:26-39

Illustration

We cannot create peace but we can accept it. Peace is a gift from God to us. We can accept it by living in a peaceful way. The mind can often be in turmoil like a raging sea and yet God is there and offering us his peace. Peace is not an absence of activity but rather a working in harmony with the world around us. Peace comes through a right relationship between others and us, but, above all, between God and us. Peace is God's gift and will help us to get back in tune with everything, but if we persist in staying out of tune with others or the world it is hard for God's peace to get to work in us.

179 Proclaiming the story

Aim

To see Jesus as the risen Lord on the shore of Galilee.

Reading

John 21:1-19

Illustration

It is told that when Jesus returned to heaven, the Archangel Michael barred his way. The archangel said, 'How can you return to heaven? Your work is not yet completed. There are many who do not know about or who have not heard of your saving acts.' Jesus said, 'I have left my friends to complete what I have begun.' The Archangel was amazed. 'Do you mean those puny, often straying humans?' 'Yes,' said Jesus, 'I trust them and I know that through following me they will bring my gospel to all the world.'

180 Humbly open to God

Aim

To encourage people to make contact with Jesus.

Reading

Luke 7:36–8:3

Illustration

Someone was described as 'a self-made man worshipping his own creator'. Think about this for a moment. Often what keeps a person from God is the illusion of self-sufficiency. Some say they have grown up and do not need such a Father figure. Yet none of us will survive without God. The strange thing is the closer someone comes to God, the more aware they are of their own weakness and sin. St Paul spoke of sinners and said, '. . . of whom I am the chief'. St Francis said, 'There is nowhere a more wretched sinner than I.' God can deal with those who are aware of their sins. He can reach out to them in forgiveness. He can reveal his love in accepting the sinner. The self-righteous and the self-sufficient set up their own barriers and are far harder to approach. Those who come to God aware of their sin and weakness are the ones who discover his power in their lives and his love.

Topical Index

Numbers refer to Illustrations and not to pagination.

Abraham 41
Absent-minded professor 69
Abundance 35, 89
Acceptance 109
Advent 1, 2, 147
Aidan 121
Airport 92
Aladdin 36
Alcoholism 100
All Saints 164, 169
Analysis 158
Andrew (Apostle) 124
Angels 19, 41
Angelus Silesius 63
Anger 128
Anointing 56
Anxiety 20
Appleseed, Johnny 155
Appreciation 141
Ascension 23, 34, 53
Attention 18, 144
Augustus 55
Awe 72

Baptism 105
Batteries 59
Battle of Hastings 13
Beach 153, 157
Beatitudes 80
Bede 121
Belief 28
Bethany 56
Bethlehem 55
Bird 72
Birdwatching 98
Blind 73
Bloom, Anthony 57
Bonhoeffer, Dietrich 166
Bored 111
Box 39
Breath 11
Bus 42
Busy 3

Calcutta 96
Cancer Research 83
Challenge 154
Chapman, Jonathan 155
Charging/recharging 59
Chemicals 158
Choice 37
Chosen 152
Christ the King 94, 99
Christmas 3, 4, 6, 143
Church 124, 159
Cinderella 118
Civil rights 148
Clover 93
Columbanus 138, 149
Coming 147
Coming of Christ 47
Complacency 168
Contact 60
Control 42
Conversion 151
Creation 72
Creation/care for 20, 141
Criticism 118
Crucifixion 110
Cuthbert 95

Damien, Father 97
Darkness 12, 21, 29, 39, 101, 104, 110, 126, 127
Dead Sea 175
Dead Sea Scrolls 137

Death and beyond 116, 117, 119
Defeat 10
Departure 92
Desert (Minnie Louise Haskins) 104
Desert Fathers 129
Devil 120, 138
Direction 104
Disasters 92
Disciples 124, 125
Discipleship 149
Dog 40
Door 156
Drained 89
Driving 150
Drugs 115

Easter 10
Ecology 35, 72
Eden 44
Emptiness 76, 101, 106
Empty 88, 111
End of world 92
Energy 35, 59
Epiphany 7, 52
Ethiopian 151
Evangelism 124, 134, 135, 151, 155
Exclusivity 27
Explosion 110

Faith 21, 57, 166, 171, 172, 177
Faithful 40
Fall 46
Family 3
Fate 53
Fear 25, 92
Fellini, Federico 101
Fish 32, 67
Flute 132
Fog 12
Follow 74
Food 158
Football 150
Force 37, 156
Forgiveness 79, 108, 128
Foundations 133
Fourth wise man 161
Frankincense 52, 123
Freedom 52, 122, 156, 175
Friend 60
Friendship 79, 128
Full 88, 111
Future 73

Gandhi 99
Gardening 8
General 38
Generosity 161
Generosity 77, 78, 139, 143
Gift 4, 6, 37, 145, 162
Giving 83, 84, 165, 175
God around us 32
God's call 74, 149, 160
God's gift 6
God's greatness 153
Godless 159
Gold 52, 87, 123
Gold, frankincense and myrrh 52, 123
Good News 29, 122, 134,
Grace 166
Great Expectations (Charles Dickens) 79
Greed 87

Happiness 85, 86
Harry Potter and the Philosopher's Stone (J. K. Rowling) 16
Hatred 27, 128
Healing 91, 112, 118
Heaven 18, 78
Hebridean Altars (Alistair Maclean) 29

Helicopter 34
Hell 78, 120
Help 40, 140, 147, 161
Hiding 154
Hole 153
Holiness 66
Holy Spirit 11, 35, 70, 88, 132
Hospitality 41, 77
Hostility 77
Hound of Heaven, The
(Francis Thompson) 76, 106
Household chores 131
Hunt, Holman 44, 156
Hypocrisy 61

India 32
Invitation 109
Iona Community 22
iPod 64

Jesus 3, 36, 42, 150
Jethro 103
John the Baptist 17, 54
Joseph, husband of Mary 122
Josephus 17
Journey 17, 24, 104, 123
Judas 56, 128
Julian of Norwich 26, 36
Julius Caesar 74

Kagawa, Toyohiko 163
King, Martin Luther 148
Kingdom of God/
Heaven 37, 42
Knock 156

Lama 113
Lamb 103
Lamp 36
Lantern Saints 164
Last Supper 128
Law 71, 115
Law and Grace 53
Lazarus 102
Lazarus and the rich man 82
Lazy 9
Leading 73
Leaving home 160
Legalism 71
Lent 8
Leprosy 97
Life 11, 12, 89
Lifeboats 26
Lift up 34
Light 12, 18, 30, 39, 90, 104,
110, 127, 134, 164
Lincoln, Abraham 173
Listen 58
Listen, refusing to 72
Listening 64, 68, 176
Little Prince 82
Little Women
(Louisa May Alcott) 143
Lonely 3
'Long spoons' 78
Lord's Prayer 67
Lost 33, 38
Love 16, 56, 62, 75, 96, 97, 110,
131, 146, 165

Magnificat 87
Magoo, Mr 73
Martin the Cobbler 47
Martin, St 165
Martyrs 142
Mary of Bethany 56
Mary, mother of Jesus 87, 122
Matheson, George 177
Message 10
Methodists 164
Michael, Archangel 179
Midas 87
Mind 153
Miners 14
Miracle on the River Kwai
(Ernest Gordon) 75

Miracle of water into wine 100
Missionary 134, 135, 138
Morning 31
Moses 103
Mother 3, 15, 16, 96, 149, 160
Music 132
Muslim 40
Myrrh 52, 123

Napoleon 10
Nativity 55
Needs 146
Neglect 3, 141
Neighbour 78, 143, 146
Nicodemus 101

Obedience 149, 160
Oliver! 152
Opportunity 74
Oppression 122
Others' needs 75

Pain 52, 56
Pasha 112
Patrick, St 93
Peace, inner 45, 86, 178
Pentecost 35, 70
Perseverance 65, 168
Philip 151
Picasso, Pablo 120
Pilgrim's Progress, The
(John Bunyan) 107
Pollution 72
Poor, The 121, 146, 161, 163
Power 35, 36, 51, 60, 70, 94, 99
Prayer 43, 60, 61, 65, 66, 67, 98, 152
Prejudice 159
Preparation 17, 54, 55
Prepare 2
Presence of God 21, 24, 46, 47, 50, 51, 53, 57, 67, 97
Prince of Peace 130
Prison 48
Procrastination 120
Promised Land 148
Punishment 37

Quirinius 55

Radio 68
Ready 2, 3
Recognise/
see, failure to 1, 4, 5, 147
Renewal 31, 53, 59, 116, 117
Representative 152
Rescue 34, 40, 42, 147, 157
Responsibility 8
Resurrection 10, 12, 13, 14, 33, 34, 102
Resuscitation 11
Reward 139
Rich young man 85
Risk 154
Rules 150

Sacrifice 33, 71, 161
Safety 154
Salvation 94, 113
Sarah 41
Save (see rescue)
Science fiction 94
Scientist 158
Scotland 91
Sea 45, 153
Sea of Galilee 175
Searching 49, 172
Security 154
Seed 9, 155
Seek 33, 38, 161
Self-giving 6, 62, 162
Selfish Giant 77
Service 163
Shackleton, Ernest 24
Shakespeare 74
Shamrock 93

Sharing 78
Sheep 33, 38, 103
Shepherd 33, 38
Shine 30, 39
Sight 5, 73
Simeon 98
Sin 27
Singh, Sundar 113
Small 153
Socrates 74, 125
Soldiers 38
Solomon, King 17
Something beautiful for God 96
Sowing 9, 155
Sparrows 25
Spirit 132
Spreading God's word 127
St Catherine 142
Starfish 157
Starvation 158
Stewardship 81
Stir up 2
Storms 36, 45
Storms of life 26
Stranger 22, 41
Strength 59
Success 81, 86, 168
Sun 90

Talents 145, 146
Television 64, 68
Temple 150
Temptation 129, 138, 171
Tennyson 160
Teresa of Avila 65
Teresa, Mother 96
Terminal 92
Thanks 15
Tibet 113
Time 43
Touch 60
Transformation 48, 51, 53, 106, 112, 114, 115, 116, 119, 180
Treasure 137
Trial of Jesus, The (John Masefield) 23
Trinity 93, 105, 153
Trust 44
Twins 136
Tyrant 37

Unsatisfied 111
Unwelcome 159

Vandalism 141
Victory 10
Vision 5, 12, 148, 160

Waiting 2, 147
Warning 72
Water 32
Waterloo 10
Wealth 52, 106
Weeding 8
Weeds 136
Werewolves 70
Wesley, John 84, 108
Winchester Cathedral 133
Wise men 7, 17, 52
Witnessing 48, 86, 142, 169, 174, 179
Words and deeds 140
Worry 20
Worthwhile 157

Yorkshire Dales 164

Zen 63

Bible Reference Index

Numbers refer to Illustrations and not to pagination.

Genesis 15:1-12, 17, 18 172
Genesis 18:1-15 41

Exodus 2:1-7 96
Exodus 20:12 15

Deuteronomy 8:7-10 148
Deuteronomy 31:6 40
Deuteronomy 34:1-8 148

1 Samuel 3:9 58

Psalm 8 72
Psalm 18:16-19 34
Psalm 63:1 158
Psalm 103:1-5 91
Psalm 145:3 153

Proverbs 14:31 163
Proverbs 19:17 163

Isaiah 40:31 35, 59
Isaiah 53 151

Lamentations 3:22-23 31

Jeremiah 18:1-11 114

Matthew 2:1-12 7, 52, 123
Matthew 2:13-23 19
Matthew 3:1-12 17
Matthew 3:13-17 75
Matthew 4:1-11 129
Matthew 4:4 111
Matthew 4:12-23 125
Matthew 5:1-12 80
Matthew 5:14-20 127
Matthew 5:16 164
Matthew 5:17-19 150
Matthew 5:19 71
Matthew 5:43-48 128
Matthew 6:5-6 61
Matthew 6:25-34 20
Matthew 7:21-29 133
Matthew 9:9-13, 18-26 106
Matthew 9:35–10:8-23 134
Matthew 10:24-39 25
Matthew 10:40-42 77
Matthew 10:42 157
Matthew 11:2-11 121
Matthew 11:16-19, 25-30 107
Matthew 13:1-9, 18-23 135
Matthew 13:3 155
Matthew 13:24-30, 36-43 136
Matthew 13:(31-33), 44-52 137
Matthew 14:13-21 78
Matthew 14:22-33 26
Matthew 15:(10-20), 21-28 27
Matthew 16:13-20 28
Matthew 16:21-28 138
Matthew 17:1-9 21
Matthew 18:15-20 79
Matthew 18:21-35 108
Matthew 19:21-22 62
Matthew 22:36-39 62
Matthew 20:1-16 139

Matthew 21:1-11 130
Matthew 21:23-32 140
Matthew 21:33-46 141
Matthew 22:1-14 109
Matthew 22:15-22 142
Matthew 22:34-46 143
Matthew 23:23-24 71
Matthew 24:1-14 29
Matthew 24:6 92
Matthew 24:7-24 42
Matthew 24:36-44 120
Matthew 25:1-13 144
Matthew 25:14-30 145
Matthew 25:31-46 146
Matthew 25:34-40 161
Matthew 28:16-20 105

Mark 1:3 2
Mark 1:16-20 74
Mark 3:1-6 154
Mark 3:31-35 160
Mark 4: 35-41 36
Mark 5:30 60
Mark 13:35 1

Luke 1:39-55 87
Luke 1:68-79 54
Luke 2:1-14 55
Luke 2:7 3
Luke 2:22-40 98, 126
Luke 2:33-35 16
Luke 2:41-52 69
Luke 2:48-50 160
Luke 3:15-17, 21, 22 50
Luke 4:1-13 171
Luke 4:14-21 49
Luke 5:1-11 174
Luke 6:17-26 85
Luke 6:20-31 169
Luke 6:27-38 175
Luke 6:39 73
Luke 7:1-10 165
Luke 7:11-17 112
Luke 7:36–8:3 180
Luke 8:22-25 86
Luke 8:26-39 178
Luke 9:28-36 95
Luke 9:51-62 166
Luke 10:1-11, 16-20 167
Luke 10:25-37 47
Luke 10:38-42 64
Luke 11:1-13 67
Luke 12:13-21 84
Luke 12:15 111
Luke 12:32 37
Luke 12:32-40 44
Luke 13:1-9 173
Luke 13:10-17 115
Luke 14:26-27 149
Luke 15:1-10 43
Luke 15:4-7 38
Luke 16:1-3 81
Luke 16:19-31 82
Luke 17:5-10 177
Luke 17:11-19 83
Luke 18:1-8 65
Luke 18:9-14 66
Luke 19:1-10 48
Luke 19:28-40 99
Luke 20:27-38 116
Luke 21:5-19 170
Luke 21:25-36 117
Luke 23:33-43 94
Luke 24:13-35 22, 119
Luke 24:44-53 23, 53

John 1:(1-9), 10-18 18
John 1:1-14 63
John 1:1-18 68
John 1:4-5 110
John 1:9-13 147
John 1:18 5
John 1:29-42 124
John 2:1-11 51, 89, 100
John 2:11 3
John 2:13-22 150
John 3:1-17 101
John 3:16 4
John 4:5-42 76
John 4:46-54 89
John 5:2-9 89
John 6:1-14 89
John 6:16-21 89
John 6:27 111
John 6:35, 41-51 158
John 8:12 12
John 9:1-7 89
John 10:1-10 103
John 10:1-18 33
John 10:10 89
John10:22-30 176
John 11:1-44 89
John 11:1-45 102
John 12:1-8 56
John 12:24 9
John 13:31-35 97
John 14:1-14 104
John 14:15-21 131
John 14:18 40
John 14:23-29 45
John 15:1-2 8
John 16:12-15 93
John 17:(1-11), 20-26 24
John 17:20-26 46
John 19:25b-27 16
John 20:1-18 13
John 20:19-29 14
John 20:19-31 57
John 20:22 11
John 21:1-19 179

Acts 1:8 35
Acts 2:1-21 70
Acts 2:4 88
Acts 8:4+ 151
Acts 8:26-40 151
Acts 17:28 32, 158
Acts 21:1-21 132
Acts 26:19 160

Romans 6:23 6
Romans 8:18-23 42
Romans 8:18-30 122
Romans 8:35-39 42
Romans 11:33-36 153
Romans 15:13 88

1 Corinthians 3:6-9 8
1 Corinthians 13:3 162
1 Corinthians 15:45 11
1 Corinthians 15:57 10

2 Corinthians 4:6 90, 39

Ephesians 5:8 39
Ephesians 5:14 30

Philippians 2:5-11 99
Philippians 4:4-7 118

1 Thessalonians 4:16-17 110

Hebrews 7:19b 152
Hebrews 7:25 152
Hebrews 11:29–12:2 168
Hebrews 13:1-8 113
Hebrews 13:2 41

James 2:1-5 159

1 John 4:7-21 75

Revelation 3:20 156

Acknowledgements

Jesus is the way:
And I said to the man . . . (Minnie Louise Haskins), taken from a collection called *Desert*, © Minnie Louise Haskins, 1908.

Good News in dark times:
Faith on a cheerless day:
Though the dawn breaks cheerless . . . *Hebridean Altars*, (Alistair MacLean), Hodder & Stoughton, 1937.

Treasuring humanity:
I know a planet . . . (Antoine de Saint-Exupéry) from *The Little Prince* by Antoine de Saint-Exupéry.

Grace is not cheap:
Cheap grace is the deadly enemy . . . by Dietrich Bonhoeffer

The publishers wish to express their gratitude to the copyright holders who have granted permission to include their material in this book. Every effort has been made to trace the copyright holders of all quoted material and we hope that no copyright has been infringed. Apology is made and pardon sought if the contrary be the case, and a correction will be made in any reprint of this book.